EVERYDAY GUIDES
MADE EASY

AVID
PRO TOOLS
BASICS

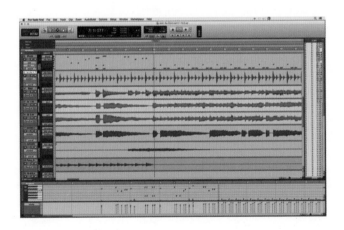

This is a **FLAME TREE** book
First published 2015

Publisher and Creative Director: Nick Wells
Project Editor: Polly Prior
Art Director and Layout Design: Mike Spender
Digital Design and Production: Chris Herbert
Copy Editor: Katharine Baker
Technical Editor: Ronan Macdonald
Proofreader: Dawn Laker
Indexer: Helen Snaith
Screenshots: Dave Clews
Picture Research: Gillian Whitaker

Special thanks to: Laura Bulbeck

This edition first published 2015 by
FLAME TREE PUBLISHING
6 Melbray Mews, 158 Hurlingham Road
London SW6 3NS
United Kingdom

www.flametreepublishing.com

15 17 19 18 16
1 3 5 7 9 10 8 6 4 2

© 2015 Flame Tree Publishing

ISBN 978-1-78361-419-6

A CIP record for this book is available from the British Library upon request.

Printed in China

All non-screenshot pictures are courtesy of © Akai Professional, LP: 32 (bottom); © Avid Technology, Inc.: 1, 6 (both), 8, 12, 16 (top), 17 (bottom), 26; © Focusrite Plc: 32 (top), 44; © KRK Systems: 33 (top); © PACE Anti-Piracy, Inc.: 14; © RØDE Microphones: 33 (left); © Sennheiser electronic GmbH & Co. KG: 33 (bottom); and Shutterstock and © the following photographers: Andresr: 22; Artpose Adam Borkowski: 123; ArtStudioHouse: 70; Be Good: 30; CREATISTA: 78; Goodluz: 126; GraphEGO: 28 (both); Stefan Holm: 13; iordani: 62; John Smith Design: 7; Cristi Kerekes: 84; klyuchnikovart: 71; Maxim_Kovalev: 80; Alexander Lukin: 83; Pepgooner: 17 (top); Pitroviz: 125; Production Perig: 119; RimDream: 87; Mihai Simonia: 5; SJ Travel Photo and Video: 3; StepanPopov: 58; Vectomart: 110; wavebreakmedia: 103

EVERYDAY GUIDES
MADE EASY

AVID
PRO TOOLS
BASICS

DAVE CLEWS

FLAME TREE
PUBLISHING

CONTENTS

All the basic information you need to take your first foray into the exciting
and inspiring world of Pro Tools.

All about choosing hardware, setting up, plugging in and getting your first
audio and MIDI recordings off the ground.

How to use Pro Tools' impressive array of editing tools to shape and polish
your recordings into finished songs.

Use the Mix window to add EQ, reverb, delay and more, while balancing volume
levels to produce a final mix.

After mixing, there is mastering: the final process of fettling your stereo mix before
releasing it to the world at large.

SERIES FOREWORD

While the unstoppable rise of computer technology has left no area of the creative arts untouched, perhaps the most profoundly transformed of them all is music. From performance, composition and production to marketing, distribution and playback, the Apple Mac and Windows PC – and, more recently, their increasingly capable smartphone and tablet cousins – have given anyone, no matter what their budget, the ability to produce professional quality tracks in the comfort of their own home and put them online for the whole world to hear.

Virtual studios such as Pro Tools (and the software instruments and effects that plug into it) put more audio and MIDI recording, editing, processing and mixing power at your fingertips than even their most well-equipped real-world counterparts could have hoped to match only 20 years ago. What's rather more difficult to come by though, is the knowledge required to put all that good stuff to use – which is where this book comes in.

A comprehensive guide, taking you through all the key concepts in a succinct, easy-to-understand way, *Avid Pro Tools Basics* is sure to serve as a trusty companion on your music-making journey, whether you're a total beginner or a more advanced producer looking to brush up on the basics. Work through it methodically from start to finish, or keep it by your side for reference – just don't forget to give us a credit on your debut album.

Ronan Macdonald
Music technology writer and editor

INTRODUCTION

Avid Pro Tools is one of the foremost digital audio workstations on the planet, used in thousands of professional studios worldwide. This book gives you all the knowledge you need to get up and running with it.

NEED TO KNOW

Filled with practical advice, this book will guide you through the basics of setting up, recording, editing, mixing and mastering with Pro Tools, explaining each process in plain English, and offering plenty of hints and tips to help you on your way to becoming a Pro Tools power user.

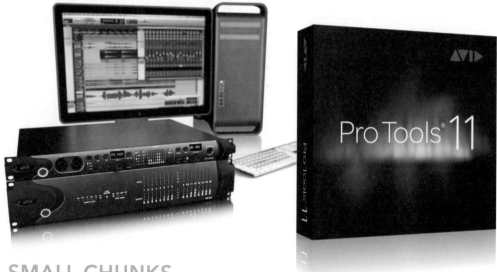

SMALL CHUNKS

There's a lot to cover, so we've boiled the information down to the essentials. Each chapter is broken up into short sections, keeping everything clear and succinct, and enabling you to dip in and out as you see fit.

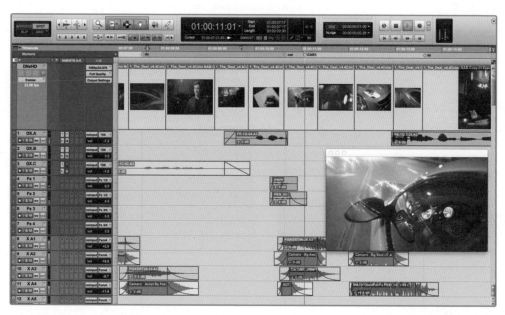

Above: Even basic Pro Tools hardware and software systems let users record up to 18 tracks.

STEP-BY-STEP GUIDES

These walk you through a range of specific techniques, from working with playlists to inserting effects plug-ins.

Hot Tips

Look out for Hot Tips throughout the book – bite-size techniques and ideas to try and to consider.

FIVE CHAPTERS

This book is divided into five chapters. The first is something of an all-round introduction to Pro Tools and the basic concepts under which it operates. The second covers everything you need to get your recordings off the ground, while the third walks you through the basics of arranging and editing your recorded material into finished tracks. Following on from this, the fourth chapter demystifies the mixing process by showing you how to add effects, balance levels and use automation, while the final chapter looks at mastering, the last process your song goes through before you share it with the world at large.

INTRODUCING PRO TOOLS

Thanks to this remarkable piece of software, it's never been easier to craft professional-sounding music that puts you on a par with the pros.

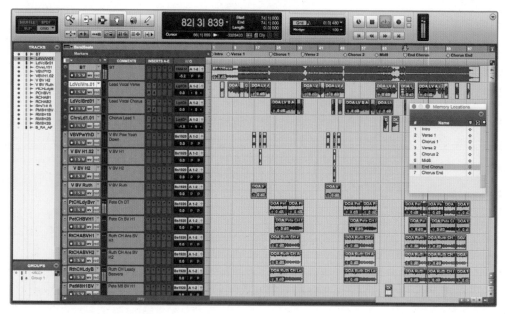

Above: A Pro Tools 11 session in full flow.

WHAT IS PRO TOOLS?

Pro Tools is a professional-standard digital audio workstation (DAW) application, which enables you to record, mix and edit audio files and MIDI data to produce either commercial-standard music or audio post-production soundtracks for film and television. It's been around for many years, starting out as Digidesign's Sound Tools in 1989, at which point it was a relatively rudimentary suite of editing tools for manipulating stereo audio files. Over time, it has evolved into an incredibly powerful digital multitrack recorder and editor, which along the way has added MIDI functionality and support for virtual instruments and video playback, transforming it into arguably the most powerful audio production resource on the planet, used in thousands of pro recording studios across the globe.

PRO POPULARITY

One of the reasons Pro Tools is so popular with professional engineers and producers is that it has always been designed around the premise of a digital tape machine mated to the computer-based equivalent of an analogue mixing console. This makes it very approachable for anyone who has ever worked in a studio containing a traditional reel-to-reel, multitrack tape machine and analogue desk set-up. It takes the concepts that have been instilled in music engineers for decades and builds on them with technologies such as elastic audio and virtual software instruments to produce a cutting-edge and powerful production environment that still somehow feels familiar. That's why the pros love it, and after reading this book, hopefully you will too.

Above: Pro Tools' Mix window is laid out like a traditional analogue mixing console.

VERSION THERAPY

Pro Tools comes in various flavours, according to your budget and/or recording requirements. How do you decide which version is right for you?

WHICH VERSION?

When it comes to running Pro Tools, there are two main options to choose from. You can run the standard Pro Tools, using the processing power of your computer to run up to 96 audio tracks, virtual instruments and effects plug-ins. Alternatively, if you pair Pro Tools HD software with one or more Avid Pro Tools HD interfaces and DSP cards, you can run sessions up to a maximum of 768 audio tracks and take full advantage of all the high-end features found in the HD version of the software. These include 7.1 surround mixing, advanced video editing and 17 different types of audio metering.

PRO TOOLS HD

The top-of-the-range option, Pro Tools HD is aimed at professional users who need high track counts, ultimate performance and surround sound capability. It comes bundled as part of a Pro Tools HDX or HD native system bundle, but can also be used without any extra hardware at all if required.

PRO TOOLS

The standard version of Pro Tools can be purchased either on its own or as part of an Avid Duet, Quartet,

Above: A Pro Tools 11 HDX system, including external DSP card and multichannel audio interface.

Mbox or Eleven Rack bundle. Lacking just a few of the high-end specs and features of the HD version, this is nonetheless a powerful package, with a maximum track count of 96 stereo tracks at a 48 kHz sample rate, or 24 tracks at 192 kHz.

PRO TOOLS EXPRESS

Pro Tools Express offers the essential features of the software in a budget solution that comes bundled free of charge when you purchase an Avid Mbox, Fast Track Solo or Fast Track Duo audio interface. It maxes out at 16 mono or stereo audio tracks, and eight instrument tracks.

PRO TOOLS FIRST

Just as this book went to press, a free, entry-level version of Pro Tools was announced under the name Pro Tools First. Providing a neat way for new users to dip their toes into the Pro Tools waters, this cut-down, 16-track option enables you to store a maximum of three projects in the cloud, with the option to purchase additional projects from the Avid Store.

Mac or PC?

Early versions of Pro Tools were Mac-only, so the Apple system has traditionally been the platform of choice for many long-term users. In these enlightened days of cross-platform compatibility, however, there's no operational difference to speak of between the Mac and PC versions, so users can go with whichever platform suits them best. All the screenshots in this book were produced on a MacBook Pro, running Pro Tools HD 11.3 under OS X 10.10.1.

Hot Tip

If a full HDX system is beyond your budget, start with a Native system. You can always upgrade later on for less than the cost of a complete new system.

Above: Cross-platform compatibility has long ceased to be an issue.

AUTHORIZATION

Pro Tools comes either as a download or on a DVD, and installs much like any other application, with a series of steps to click through. Once that's done, you're ready to begin the authorization process.

UNDER iLOK AND KEY

To combat software piracy, Pro Tools uses a USB hardware dongle called an iLok, which must be inserted while Pro Tools is running. Depending on which bundle you purchase, you may get an iLok included in the package, or you may need to buy one separately for around £30.

Below: Pro Tools requires hardware copy protection in the form of an iLok2 USB key.

Hot Tip

When downloading, don't forget to grab an extra 2.3 GB of bundled plug-ins and sounds (the AIR Creative Collection) alongside Pro Tools itself.

Copy Protection

The iLok acts as a portable container for your Pro Tools licence, an encrypted software document that's a little like a digital receipt. To run your copy of Pro Tools, your licence needs to be transferred to your iLok via the ilok.com website, so you first need to set up an ilok.com account.

THE iLOK AUTHORIZATION MANAGER

It's easy to authorize your iLok licence.

1. Once you've navigated to www.ilok.com and registered your details to create a free account, download and install the iLok License Manager app on to your computer.

2. Once this is launched, log in with your iLok.com account details and you can access your account. You should be able to see your Pro Tools licence in the list of available licences.

Above: Use the iLok License Manager to activate your Pro Tools licence.

3. Click to select the licence in the list and you should see the details appear in the lower window. Click on Activate and select the appropriate iLok in the dialogue box that appears.

4. Click OK to transfer the licence to the iLok. Your Pro Tools software should now be ready to use as long as you have that iLok inserted into a USB slot.

BASIC CONCEPTS

At the heart of Pro Tools lie a few basic concepts to get to grips with. Here's a jargon-free breakdown to get you up to speed.

AUDIO ENGINE

An audio engine is a special piece of software designed to stream audio data from your computer's memory and hard drive to your audio interface efficiently. Pro Tools can use multiple types of audio engine. The Avid Audio Engine (AAE) is for use with Avid's own hardware interfaces; Core Audio is for Mac systems with non-Avid interfaces; and ASIO is for use with non-Avid Windows systems.

Left: Pro Tools now features a 64-bit audio engine.

HARD DISK RECORDING

This is Pro Tools' raison d'être – the practice of capturing audio and storing it digitally on to a hard disk for playback. It enables you to dip into a recording instantly at any point, with no rewinding or fast-forwarding required.

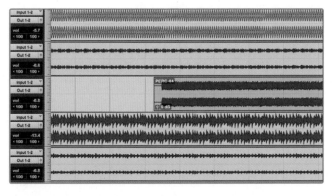

Above: Hard-disk recording allows instant access to any point in the track.

MIDI

MIDI stands for Musical Instrument Digital Interface, and it has been allowing synthesizers and computers to communicate since 1984. It transmits information such as note length and position, pitch and velocity. Pro Tools boasts a fully featured set of MIDI tools, allowing performances to be captured from input devices such as MIDI keyboards and played back via hardware or software instruments.

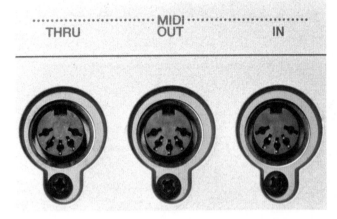

Above: MIDI has been with us for a while, and it's still going strong.

NATIVE PROCESSING

Host-based or native processing is what happens when all of the calculations required to run audio playback, virtual instruments and effects are done by the computer's own built-in processor(s), rather than on dedicated external digital signal processing (DSP) cards.

Right: Native processing means you can now run Pro Tools on just a laptop.

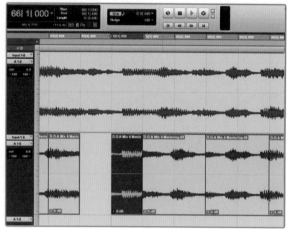

NON-DESTRUCTIVE EDITING

Also known as non-linear editing, this refers to the way in which Pro Tools enables you to chop up and rearrange recorded material without affecting the source audio files stored on your hard disk. Any edits you make in the software simply determine the order in which the data is played back from the disk.

Left: Non-destructive editing gives you the power to chop up your audio with abandon.

Below: Pro Tools supports a veritable cornucopia of sample rates.

SAMPLE RATES

Any digital audio system is based on sampling incoming audio, which means cutting it into tiny slices several thousand times per second and storing these slices as a stream of data. The sample rate is the number of samples captured per second, and is thus measured in kilohertz. Pro Tools supports sample rates from 8 kHz up to 192 kHz.

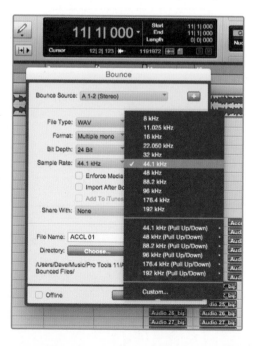

Hot Tip

Don't be too tempted by high sample rates, as the trade-off is enormous audio file sizes. For general usage, you shouldn't need to go higher than 24-bit/96 kHz.

SYSTEM RESOURCES

Each computer system that runs Pro Tools has a finite number of system resources. The number of tracks, virtual instruments and effects plug-ins you can run at once is dependent on how much processing power your system has available. For instance, a Mac Pro with two Pro Tools HDX cards installed could run much more complex sessions than a MacBook Pro with no additional hardware attached.

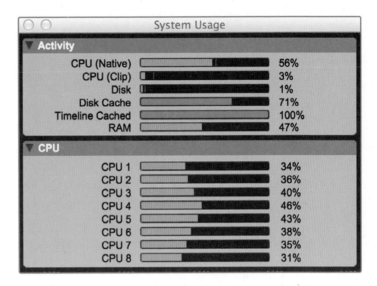

Above: The System Usage window gives you an at-a-glance view of how your resources are holding out.

SESSIONS

Each new Pro Tools project you create is known as a session file, saved with the file extension .ptx. Session files contain information relating to the contents of the Edit window and the state of the Mix window, automation data and effects settings. They don't contain actual audio files, however – these are stored in a separate Audio Files folder on your hard drive.

Left: Session files and audio files are stored separately in the session folder on your hard drive.

THE PRO TOOLS INTERFACE

Pro Tools operates in two main windows – the Edit window and the Mix window. Here's a quick tour of the important bits of each.

THE EDIT WINDOW

The Edit window is where you do most of your recording, editing and arranging, so you'll be spending a lot of time here.

1. **Edit Mode Buttons**: The four Edit modes (Shuffle, Spot, Slip and Grid) govern how audio clips can be moved in the timeline. Clips either snap on to the ends of adjacent clips (Shuffle), snap to a specific location (Spot), move around freely (Slip) or snap to the Bars & Beats grid (Grid).

2. **Zoom Buttons**: These enable you to zoom in and out for a better view of tracks in the timeline, both horizontally and vertically. You can also store five zoom settings as recallable snapshots for quick access to your favourite views.

3. **Editing Tools**: The three main editing tools – the Trim, Selector and Grabber tools – can be combined into a single Smart tool that adopts the required function according to where you place the cursor on a clip. More about these on pages 62–64.

4. **Counter Display**: This displays your current location in the track. The primary and secondary counters can both be set to display SMPTE timecode, minutes and seconds, bars and beats, or even individual samples. The display also shows the current edit selection range.

5. **Transport Controls**: Like the buttons on a tape machine, these enable you to record, play, stop, fast-forward and rewind within your session.

⑥ **Timeline Area**: The main area of the Edit window is where you move, chop, edit and copy audio and MIDI clips to make your song or track.

⑦ **Tracks**: Like the tracks on a multitrack tape machine, each horizontal row can play back either one track of audio or a single MIDI part. The track headers on the left of the screen contain level meters and controls for naming and setting what each track displays, as well as its record, mute or solo status.

⑧ **Automation**: Automation curves can be viewed for each track. These are continuous, editable lines denoting the position of a particular control or effect setting at any point during the track. This enables you to vary that track's volume level or pan setting over time, for example.

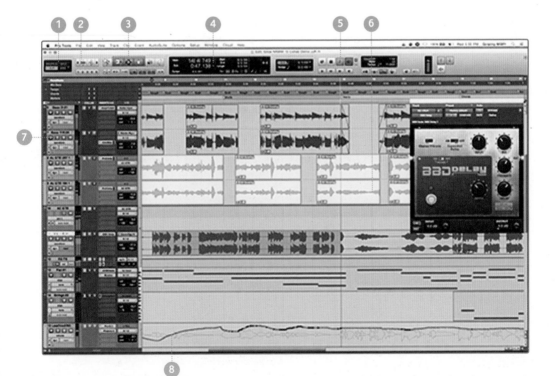

THE MIX WINDOW

The Mix window is where you add effects and balance each track's level and pan position, bringing everything together into one cohesive mix.

1 **Track List**: Appearing in both the Edit and Mix windows, this list of all the tracks in the session makes it easy to quickly find, select, hide and reposition tracks.

2 **Channel Strips**: Unlike the Edit window's horizontal tracks, each track is represented in the Mix window by a vertical channel strip, like you'd find on a mixing desk.

3 **Instrument View**: These slots house any virtual software instruments that are loaded into the track, such as Xpand!2 or the Vacuum monosynth.

4 **Inserts View**: These slots are where you insert effects plug-ins across the channel. Each channel has 10 slots, viewable in blocks of five, labelled A to E and F to J.

5 **Sends View**: These slots are where you configure sends, which are controls that send variable levels of the signal in that channel to other parts of the mixer.

Hot Tip

Switch between the Edit and Mix windows quickly by holding down the Command key (Mac; Control on a PC) and pressing the = key.

⑥ **Routing & Automation:** This section is where you can set the input source and output destination for each track, as well as adjust its automation mode.

⑦ **Pan Pots:** These knobs control the channel's position in the stereo image. Turn fully left to send the sound to the left speaker, fully right to send to the right speaker, or anywhere in between.

⑧ **Channel Faders:** Replicating the vertical faders found on mixing consoles, these are essentially volume controls for each track in your session. Pull down to make quieter, push up to make louder.

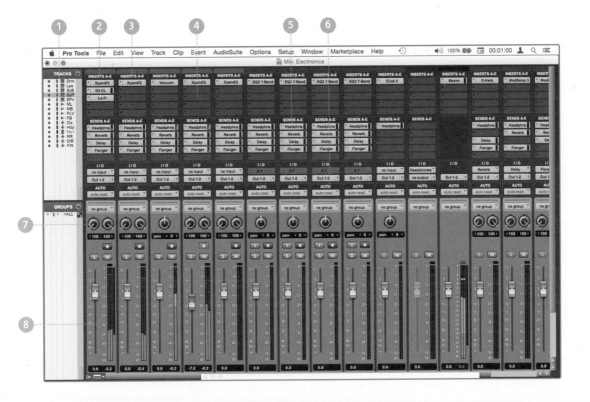

TRACK TYPES

A Pro Tools project can contain a number of different types of track. Here's a brief overview of what they all do.

AUDIO TRACK

The most important track type is the audio track. This contains audio clips that are played back from your hard drive.

MIDI TRACK

MIDI tracks are used to record, store and play back note data to external MIDI devices, such as hardware synths and samplers.

INSTRUMENT TRACK

Instrument tracks also contain MIDI data, but unlike MIDI tracks, they're used to play software instruments within Pro Tools.

AUXILIARY INPUT TRACK

Auxiliary (aux) tracks can be used as containers for effects plug-ins or inputs from external hardware instruments. Audio can also be routed to them from other channels.

VIDEO TRACK

Video tracks enable you to import QuickTime or Windows Media Video (WMV) video files and play them back in the Edit window.

MASTER FADER TRACK

Like the master fader on a mixing desk, these act as level controls for combined signals that are routed to a physical output, such as your audio interface's main stereo output. Usually all the channels in your Pro Tools mixer are combined and routed through a Master Fader track. The meters on the channel are the ones to watch for clipping as you mix the track.

VCA GROUP TRACK

Found only in Pro Tools HD, these are used to control the level of groups of faders. Useful for putting all the drum channels on to a single fader, for example.

PLUG-INS

Plug-ins are extra pieces of software, usually virtual instruments or audio effects, that can be 'plugged in' to a host application, such Pro Tools, to extend its functionality.

AAX PLUG-INS

Standing for Avid Audio eXtension, AAX is the latest plug-in format supported by Pro Tools, replacing the venerable TDM and RTAS formats supported by systems of yesteryear. Devised to be compatible with 64-bit systems, the format comes in three varieties.

AAX DSP

Designed to take advantage of the extra DSP (digital signal processing) chips found on HDX hardware cards, the AAX DSP format is compatible with Pro Tools HDX systems only.

AAX Native

Intended to use the host computer's CPU (central processing unit) for its DSP processing, the AAX Native

Left: Pro Tools now uses the 64-bit AAX plug-in format.

format is compatible with either Pro Tools or Pro Tools HD from version 10 upwards. Both AAX DSP and AAX Native plug-ins operate in real time, with no processing time required.

AAX Audiosuite

Traditionally, Audiosuite plug-ins were used to process audio offline, as opposed to in real time. After using a Preview mode to hear the effect of the plug-in, you would hit a Render button and a new audio file would be created and pasted into the session in place of the original version.

To bring Audiosuite into line with the 64-bit Pro Tools 11, AAX Audiosuite has been introduced, and it still operates in the same way, as opposed to AAX DSP and AAX Native plug-ins, which operate in real time.

Left: AAX Audiosuite plug-ins do their processing offline as opposed to in real time.

FILE FORMATS

Pro Tools works with a variety of audio file types. Here's the lowdown on the ones you're most likely to be using day to day.

COMPATIBILITY AND EXPORT OPTIONS

Most of the time, the audio you'll be working with in your Pro Tools sessions will be in one of two formats: WAV or AIFF.

WAV

Compatible with both Windows and Mac platforms, the WAV file is probably the most widely used audio file format today. Pro Tools uses a form of WAV file known as BWF (Broadcast Wave Format), specifically developed for use in broadcast audio and video applications.

AIFF

Short for Audio Interchange File Format, AIFF is a non-compressed file format originally developed by Apple, although AIFF files are now compatible with Windows platforms, too.

Neither WAV nor AIFF files need to be converted for use in Pro Tools, and both types are available as export options, along with the MP3 format.

Above: WAV and AIFF are the two main audio file formats supported by Pro Tools.

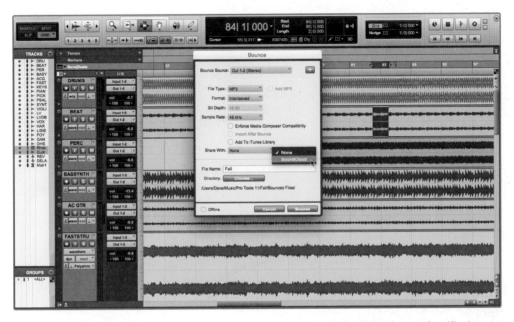

Above: Export your finished tracks directly to your SoundCloud account.

MP3

The MP3 format is famous (some would say infamous) for being the compression format that allows easy file sharing due to the small size of the audio files it creates. MP3 files are extremely widely supported on platforms such as iTunes, iPhones and almost every other mobile music player and smartphone on the planet.

MP3 files are also great for fast uploading to services such as SoundCloud to get your music heard by a large online community. As luck would have it, Pro Tools 11 offers direct export to SoundCloud as an option in its Bounce to Disk window.

MXF

Media Exchange Format (MXF) files are designed to be easily interchangeable between media servers in professional audio-visual facilities, so their use is beyond the remit of this book.

RECORDING

GEARING UP

As well as your computer and a copy of Pro Tools, there are one or two other things you need before you can start making music.

AUDIO INTERFACE

An audio interface is essential for getting sound from microphones and instruments, such as electric guitars, into Pro Tools. These days, you can use pretty much any third-party audio interface to get sound in and out of your system. Budget USB interfaces are abundant, and quality items can be had for around the £100 mark.

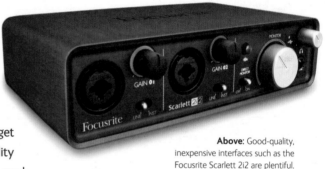

Above: Good-quality, inexpensive interfaces such as the Focusrite Scarlett 2i2 are plentiful.

MIDI CONTROLLER KEYBOARD

MIDI keyboards fall into two categories: those with USB ports and those that have old-style five-pin DIN MIDI ports (some models still offer both types). USB keyboards can be plugged directly into a USB port on your computer, but five-pin DIN-equipped models need a separate MIDI interface to connect to the computer.

Above: Akai's MPK249 USB MIDI controller features drum pads, faders and rotary knobs, as well as a musical keyboard.

MONITORS

A good pair of monitor speakers is a must for programming and mixing. The small nearfield type are usually best for small rooms, and active speakers that have built-in amplifiers are a great idea, because they don't require a separate power amp to drive them.

MICROPHONE

If you're going to be recording any vocals or acoustic instruments, you need a decent microphone. Large-capsule condenser designs make the best all-rounders, and you can choose either a standard mic that plugs into your audio interface, or a USB model that plugs into your computer's USB port.

Above: KRK's Rokit RP5 G3 active nearfield monitors, with their distinctive yellow cones, are a popular pro studio choice.

Above: The Rode NT1-A, seen here with optional pop shield and shockmount, is renowned as the world's quietest studio mic.

Right: Sennheiser's HD-25 headphones are comfortable and easy to listen to for long periods, making them ideal studio companions.

HEADPHONES

Essential when recording with microphones, a decent pair of closed-back headphones are good for working at night (so you don't disturb the neighbours) and for revealing small details that don't show up so well on speakers.

SETTING UP

When it comes to what plugs in where, things can become a little confusing. Here's a basic guide to hooking it all up.

CONNECTING HARDWARE

These days, it's not necessary to purchase thousands of pounds' worth of expensive hardware interfaces and DSP cards to be able to run a Pro Tools system. Thanks to today's fast, powerful CPU chips, you can easily run a basic, budget system with nothing more than a laptop, a small USB audio interface and a decent pair of monitor speakers. Oh, and a few instruments to actually record. Here's a diagram of how it all fits together.

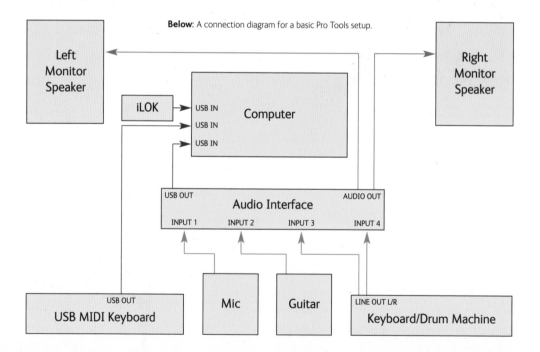

Below: A connection diagram for a basic Pro Tools setup.

CONFIGURING YOUR INTERFACE

When you launch Pro Tools for the first time, you need to tell it what audio interfaces you have connected and how their inputs and outputs will be labelled.

1. Choose the Playback Engine option from the Setup menu and select your interface from the topmost pop-up. Click OK – your session is closed and then reloaded in the background.

2. Next, from the Setup menu once again, choose the I/O option. Click on the Input tab and delete the existing path by clicking on its name and hitting the Backspace key. Then do the same in the Output tab to delete the existing output path.

3. Hold down the Alt/Option (on a Mac) or Alt (on a PC) key and click the Default button. This creates new input and output paths for the interface you assigned in Step 1. Double-click the names of these new paths to relabel them.

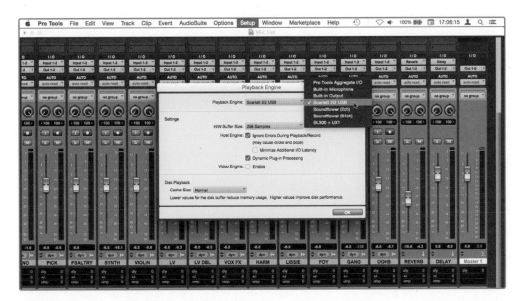

Above: Setting an interface in the Playback Engine window.

RECORDING IN PRO TOOLS

You're all set up, connected and ready to rock – so what now?
Here's how to create a new session and get your first tracks recorded.

CREATING A NEW SESSION

When you first launch Pro Tools, the first thing you see is the Quick Start window. This enables you to create either a new session from a template or a new blank session, or open an existing session – just click the required button to select your preferred option. For best compatibility, begin by choosing the BWF (.WAV) Audio File Type, with a bit depth of 24 Bit and a sample rate of 44.1 kHz. Leave the I/O Settings set to Last Used for now, then click OK to create the session file.

Below: The Pro Tools HD Quick Start window.

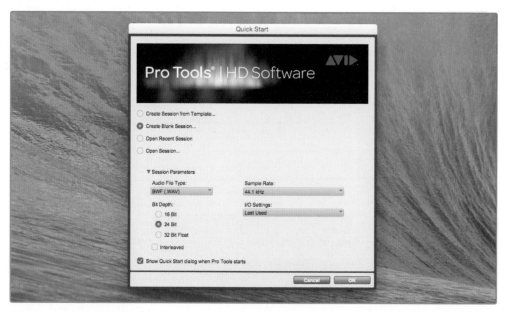

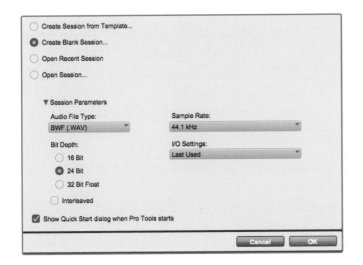

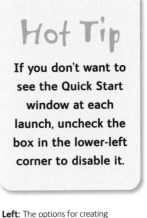

Hot Tip

If you don't want to see the Quick Start window at each launch, uncheck the box in the lower-left corner to disable it.

Left: The options for creating a new session.

Templates

Pro Tools includes specially pre-installed template sessions designed to act as starting points for new projects. They can be accessed by clicking the Create Session From Template button.

Bit Depth

Bit depth is to do with the audio's dynamic range – the difference between the loudest and quietest signals; 16-bit yields a potential dynamic range of 96 dB, while 24-bit gives you 144 dB, delivering a lot more headroom.

Audio File Type

Pro Tools gives you the choice between BWF (.WAV) and AIFF file types. It's usually best to go with BWF, because of its widespread compatibility.

Sample Rate

As explained on page 18, the sample rate is the number of audio samples captured per second. It's a measure of resolution, like the megapixel count on a digital camera. CDs use a sample rate of 44.1 kHz.

NAMING AND SAVING

Pro Tools session files are saved on to your computer's hard disk, so you need to give each session a name that will help you keep track of it.

Making a Session File

Here is how to make your first session file:

1. After choosing your blank session settings in the Quick Start window, click OK.

2. In the subsequent dialogue box, select a location on your hard drive in which to save the session. Give it a suitable name and hit Save.

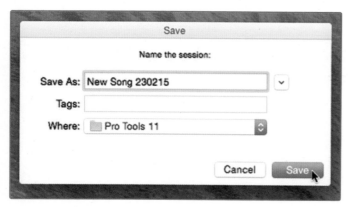

Above: Naming and saving a new session.

> ## Hot Tip
>
> Each time you save your session, rename it to keep track of subsequent versions of your song as you work on it – for example, 'SPRING 08 Recording Vocals'.

3. Decide on a tempo for the project, in beats per minute (bpm). Click the small red diamond at the left edge of the green tempo ruler and enter the desired tempo. Click OK.

4. Bring up the New Track window by choosing the New... option from the Track menu. Alternatively, use the keyboard shortcut Shift + Command + N (Mac) or Shift + Control + N (PC).

CREATING A NEW AUDIO TRACK

In Pro Tools, audio is recorded on to tracks like a tape machine. The difference is that you have to create the tracks before you start recording!

Adding Blank Tracks to Your Session

You are just a few steps away from adding blank tracks to your session:

1. Choose whether you want to record a mono or stereo audio track by selecting from the first pop-up. Mono is best for vocals, instruments recorded with a single microphone and single-output instruments, such as guitar and bass. Choose stereo if you're recording a stereo keyboard or synth.

2. Make sure that Audio Track is selected as the track type, and set the In menu to Samples. This is the default timebase setting for audio tracks.

3. Enter the number of tracks required in the Quantity box on the left, then click Create. You now have your first audio track in your session.

Below: Creating a mono audio track.

THE TRACK HEADER

The box on the left-hand side of each track is called the track header. Here's a heads-up on what it contains.

WHAT YOU WILL SEE

The track header starts out in what's called minimal view, displaying only the elements shown below, but it's capable of showing you much more. Either selecting the Edit Window Views option from the View menu or clicking the small white triangle button just above the track header column reveals a list of all the possible things it can contain, if you have enough screen room. These include a comments box, input and output settings, volume and pan controls, and the insert and send slots.

1. **Track Name**
2. **Record Ready Button**
3. **Input Monitor Button**
4. **Solo Button**
5. **Mute Button**
6. **Display Selector**
7. **Voice Allocation**
8. **Automation Mode**
9. **Timebase Selector**
10. **Automation Lane**

MAKING A CLICK TRACK

Before you begin recording, you need something to keep you in time. Creating a click track gives you a steady beat to play to.

1. Select the Create Click Track option from the bottom of the Track menu.

2. The default track loads with the Click II plug-in providing the sound of the click. Press Play to hear it.

3. To change the sound of the click, flip to the Mix page and click on the Click II plug-in loaded into Insert Slot A at the top of the Click channel.

4. Click the pop-ups to the right of Click 1 and Click 2 to load a new sound for each. Click 1 plays on the downbeat, so is usually louder.

Below: Creating a click track with the Click II plug-in.

PREPARING AUDIO TRACKS

Before you begin recording on to a track, there are one or two routine things you have to do to set it up. These include selecting an input source, as well as naming and record-enabling the track.

SELECTING AN INPUT SOURCE

An input source is another name for what you'll be recording. It usually refers to the channel on your interface to which your instrument or mic is connected.

Below: Selecting an audio track's input source.

1. Click the small white triangle button just above the track header column and select I/O from the menu to reveal the input and output section of the track header.

2. Click on the Input slot to reveal a sub-menu of available interface inputs. This is where the I/O labels you created on page 35 appear.

3. Identify the input on your audio interface to which you've connected your instrument, and select this as the input for the track.

Name Your Track

It's always a good idea to name your tracks before you record on to them. This way, audio files retain the track name when they're recorded, making it easier to keep track of them later. Do this by double-clicking the Audio 1 label in the track header and typing in a new name.

> # Hot Tip
>
> **If your audio interface has no physical gain controls, look in the Hardware Setup menu under Setup, or in the software control panel it came with.**

INPUT MONITORING

Click the 'I' button in the track header to put the track into input monitoring mode. This enables you to hear the signal as it will be recorded, even while the track is playing, so you can sing or play along.

Gain Control

While singing or playing, adjust the gain control on your interface (if it has one) until the level meter on the track is full of green segments, but isn't going into the red at any point. If it does go into the red, turn the gain down to avoid the signal clipping, because this causes undesirable digital distortion.

Right: The Input Monitoring button is handy for setting levels.

SETTING LEVELS

Proper gain staging can have a profound impact on the quality of your recordings, so it's a good habit to get into.

WHAT IS GAIN STAGING?

The route that audio takes from its source (your voice or another instrument) to its destination (an audio track within Pro Tools) is known as the signal path. There are several points in the signal path at which the loudness level, or gain, can be adjusted:

○ **Guitar**: The output volume on a guitar.

○ **Guitar amp**: The input gain and master volume on a guitar amp.

○ **Audio interface**: The input gain of the mic pre-amp on your audio interface where your mic is plugged in.

Any of these points has the potential to add unwanted noise into the signal path, so at each stage, make sure the signal level is set just right by using level meters to guide you.

Below: Use your interface's gain controls to set up gain staging.

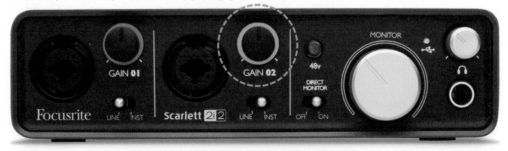

MAXIMIZE YOUR SIGNAL/NOISE RATIO

Shown to the right are three level meters displaying the level of an incoming signal to be recorded.

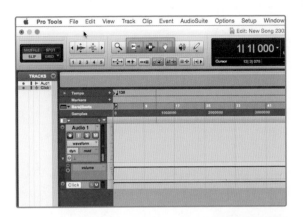

1. This level is set too low, resulting in a poor signal/noise ratio. At this level, the signal will need to be boosted at a later stage, boosting unwanted noise along with it.

2. On the other hand, this meter is going into the red, indicating that the level on this channel is set too high, introducing unwanted distortion that will be present all the way down the rest of the signal path.

3. The level displayed here is just right, resulting in a loud but clean signal with no distortion and minimal unwanted noise. Perfect.

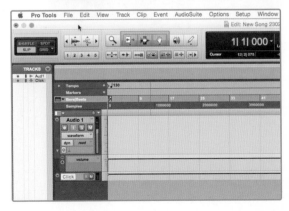

Hot Tip

If you find the red clip indicator stuck on in your level meter, use the Alt/Option + C (Mac) or Alt + C (PC) key command to reset it.

RECORDING VOCALS

In a nod to the days of reel-to-reel recording, here's a technique for squeezing the maximum number of vocal tracks out of your system.

MAKING A VOCAL SLAVE

When recording vocals for the average pop song, there's a good chance you'll need a lot of tracks for backing vocals. For this reason, many people bounce (*see page 88*) the music session down to a stereo backing track and import this stereo file into a new slave (*see page 89*) session specifically for the purpose of laying down the vocals.

Below: The average pop backing vocal session can run to dozens of tracks.

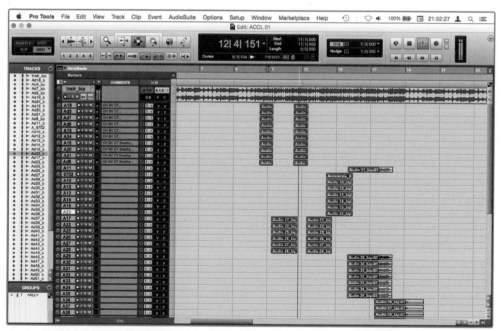

This frees up the computer's processing power immensely, and means you can happily capture a gazillion vocal parts. Multiple backing vocal tracks can then be mixed down to convenient stereo pairs and imported back into the main session later.

Slave Yourself

This is how to make a slave session:

1. Bounce a rough instrumental mix of your music track to a stereo audio file – *see page 108 for details on how to do this.*

2. Create a new blank session named 'Vocals' or similar at the same tempo as the music session. Import your backing track to a stereo audio track, starting from Bar 1, Beat 1.

3. Connect your microphone to one of the mic inputs on your audio interface, then select this input as the input of a new mono track in Pro Tools. Name the track 'Vocal'.

4. Many mics require a 48V phantom power supply to be sent from the interface down the mic cable. If yours does, remember to turn it on.

Below: A vocal slave reel showing backing track and blank vocal tracks with monitor reverb.

VOCAL RECORDING TIPS

If you're new to recording vocals, it can be quite a daunting process. Here are a few handy tips to help things run smoothly.

- **Headphones:** Connect a pair of headphones to your interface's headphone-out socket. Make sure it's set to monitor the stereo output from Pro Tools.

- **Headphone splitter:** If you're recording someone else singing, you need headphones too. If your interface only has one headphone output, use a headphone splitter so you can both listen.

- **Reverb or Delay:** Most singers like a little reverb or delay effect in their headphones. To set this up, use a reverb or delay plug-in as a bus effect (*see page 98*) and send to it from the vocal track.

- **Turn it down!** Begin the session with the level of the backing track turned down to around -10 dB. This gives plenty of headroom for the singer to be able to hear their own voice over the track.

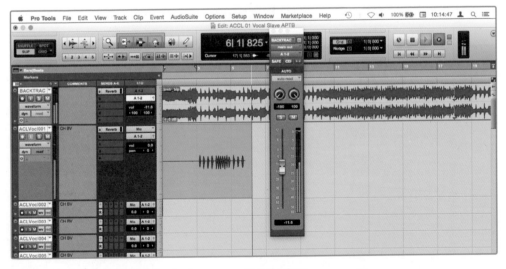

Above: Turning down the backing track gives the singer more monitoring headroom.

RECORDING GUITARS

Pro Tools has a built-in tuner plug-in called InTune. Once tuned, plug into Eleven (see below) for some great guitar tones.

Tuning Up

No need to bother with fiddly external tuners when you can just load up InTune.

1. Connect your guitar to an input on your audio interface, then select this input as the input of a new mono audio track in Pro Tools.

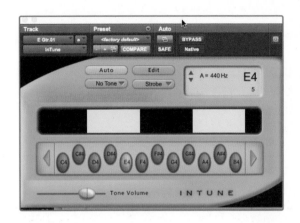

Above: InTune offers both a strobe mode and a more conventional needle mode.

2. Open the track's Inserts view and click on the first empty insert slot. You'll find InTune in the Other sub-menu. Load it up.

3. Hit a string on your guitar and adjust the tuning until the strobe bars stop moving.

Go to Eleven

Eleven Free offers a variety of realistic-sounding guitar effects.

1. In the next insert slot, load up Eleven Free from the Harmonic sub-menu.

2. Eleven is a software guitar amp simulator. Choose a preset from the Preset menu.

3. Use the control knobs to tailor the sound, as on a real amp, then rock out!

Above: Pro Tools' built-in software guitar amp really does go to Eleven.

RECORDING USING AN AUX

Using an Aux channel to route the incoming signal to an audio track means that you can capture the sounds of effects plug-ins and record them to disk.

Above: Recording an audio track through a plug-in inserted on an Aux Input track.

RECORDING A PLUG-IN

Normally, when you record directly on to an audio track, any plug-ins that you then insert on that track are passing the dry recorded signal through them and you're hearing the result. But what if you want to record the plug-in's output?

Make Your Recording

Here's how to set up an Aux Input track to record through a plug-in:

1. Create a new Aux Input track and switch its I/O view on in the track header.

2. Select the required input source and set the output to the first available bus.

3. Create a new audio track and set its input to be the bus you selected in Step 2.

4. Insert the plug-in you need into the first Insert slot of the Aux channel.

5. Record-enable the audio track. The recorded audio will be the output of the plug-in.

PUNCHING IN

Punching in means dropping Pro Tools into record at a particular point while the track is playing. This can be done manually or pre-programmed.

Punching in Manually

To punch in manually, just follow these steps:

1. Enable QuickPunch in the Options menu.

2. Record-enable the target track.

3. Set the track playing and click the Record button at the point you want to start recording.

4. Click the Record button again to stop recording.

Above: Using QuickPunch to drop in and out of record on the fly.

Programmed Punches

To set up a pre-programmed punch, this is what to do:

1. Enable QuickPunch, Link Timeline and Edit Selection in the Options menu.

2. Record-enable the target track.

3. Make a selection range with the Selector tool around the punch-in area.

4. Select Window, then Transport, and enable the Pre-roll and Post-roll buttons. Set both to two bars.

5. Click the Record button.

6. Set the track playing.

7. Pro Tools punches in and out of record in accordance with the selection range.

> **Hot Tip**
>
> By default, Pro Tools records audio to the system disk. You can select another destination in the Disk Allocation menu under Setup.

LOOP RECORDING

Also known as cycle recording, this enables you to record the same part multiple times in a continuous loop without stopping to rewind each time.

Setting Up Loop Recording

To make a loop recording, just follow these steps:

1. Select the Loop Record item from the Options menu. A loop symbol appears in the transport's Record button.

2. Click the Record Ready button in the audio track's header.

Above: Loop recording is a great way to capture multiple vocal takes seamlessly.

3. Enable the Link Timeline and Edit Selection mode in the Options menu.

4. Use the Selector tool to set the loop range by highlighting the portion of the track that you want to loop around.

5. Click the Record button in the Transport to arm Pro Tools for recording.

6. Click the Play button or tap the spacebar to begin recording.

Hot Tip

Try setting the loop range a couple of bars before and after the section you're recording. This gives you time to breathe between each pass.

MULTITRACK RECORDING

A multiple-channel audio interface can capture several tracks at once, making it ideal for recording bands or multi-mic sources, such as drum kits.

Recording on Multiple Tracks

You need an interface with more than one input to do this. Make sure all the instruments you want to record are connected to the relevant inputs.

1. Create as many blank audio tracks as you need and name them appropriately.

2. Set each track's input source to the correct interface channel.

3. Record-enable each track by clicking its Record Ready button.

4. Click the Record button in the Transport to arm Pro Tools for recording.

5. Click Play. All the tracks will begin recording.

6. Click Stop to end recording.

Below: Record a whole band at once with multitrack recording.

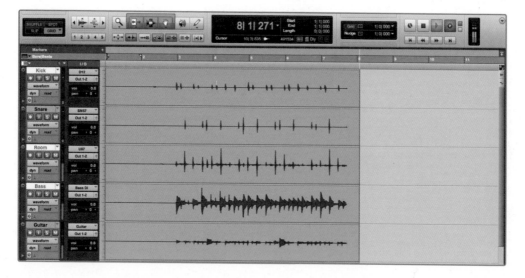

MIDI RECORDING

As well as audio, Pro Tools is a capable MIDI sequencer that works with both internal software instruments and external hardware instruments.

Above: Inserting an Xpand!2 instrument on an Instrument track.

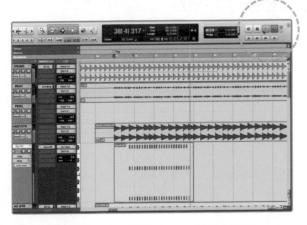

Above: Recording a MIDI part on to an Instrument track.

SOFTWARE INSTRUMENTS

Software instruments are nothing short of miraculous things, creating sound from nothing but hard maths.

1. Create a new stereo Instrument track. Click on the first insert slot in the I/O view and choose a software instrument from the menu.

2. Name the track. The MIDI clips adopt this track name after you create them.

3. Click the Record Ready button in the track header and play your MIDI keyboard controller. You should now be able to hear the instrument as you play.

4. When ready, click the Record button in the Transport, followed by the Play button. Play in your part and hit Stop when finished.

EXTERNAL INSTRUMENTS

As well as software instruments, you can also record more traditional things like synths and samplers, triggering them via Pro Tools' MIDI sequencer.

1. Connect your instrument to the appropriate line level inputs on your audio interface.

2. Connect your MIDI interface's MIDI Out to the MIDI In on your instrument.

3. Go to Setup, then MIDI, followed by MIDI Studio, and add your device.

4. Create and name a new stereo audio track in Pro Tools. Set its input to be the interface inputs you hooked up in Step 1.

5. Create a new MIDI track and set its output to the correct MIDI channel for the sound on the instrument you want to record.

6. Record-enable the audio track and play your MIDI controller. You should now be able to hear the instrument and see the track level meters moving.

7. When ready, click the Record button in the Transport, followed by the Play button. Play in your part and hit Stop when finished.

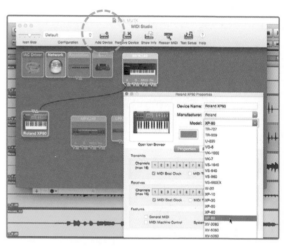

Above: Click the Add Device button in Audio MIDI Setup and select your MIDI device from the list.

Above: The devices you added in the MIDI Setup window should become available as MIDI track outputs.

IMPORTING

Pro Tools doesn't just work with material you've recorded yourself. It can work happily with files from other sources, too.

IMPORTING AUDIO FILES

Occasionally, you might get hold of a folder full of audio files that needs to be turned into a Pro Tools session. With any luck, these will have been prepared so that they all begin at the start of the song and play together as a whole piece. Files like these are known as stems. Here is how to import them:

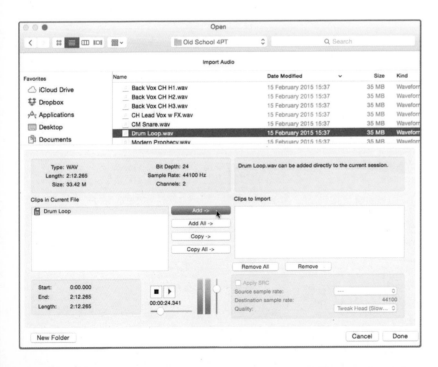

1. Create a new blank session and set the correct song tempo if you know it.

2. Go to File, then Import, followed by Audio, and use the file browser to navigate to the folder on your hard drive that contains the files in question.

Left: The Import Audio window.

3. Click on the desired files in the upper window. Use the Add or Copy buttons to transfer them into the Clips to Import window.

4. When all the required clips are selected, click Done to transfer them to your session.

5. In the Audio Import Options dialogue box, choose whether to place the files into the clip list or on to new tracks.

IMPORTING SESSION DATA

The Import Session Data command enables you to import specific tracks, complete with all settings, from other Pro Tools sessions. Here's how:

1. Under File, then Import and Session Data, select the .ptx session file that contains the required track(s) and click Open.

2. Choose the desired track from the Tracks pane, choose New Track as the destination and click OK.

Above: Choose to place imported audio on to new tracks or into the clip list.

Above: The Import Session Data window.

EDITING & ARRANGING

THE FOUR EDIT MODES

You can switch between Pro Tools' edit modes by clicking on their buttons with the mouse, hitting function keys F1 to F4, or repeatedly tapping the accent (`) key.

Above: Shuffle mode enables you to shuffle the order of clips.

Above: Slip mode enables you to slip things around freely.

SHUFFLE (F1)

Shuffle mode enables you to move, trim, delete, copy or paste clips, but their movement is constrained to other clips in the timeline. What this means is that whenever you move a clip while in Shuffle mode, it always snaps to the edge of an adjacent clip. For example, if you add a clip to the start of a track, all the other clips move along to accommodate it.

SLIP (F2)

Slip mode enables you to move and place clips freely around the timeline without snapping to anything. Use this mode for freely positioning clips, making non-restricted selections with the Selector tool or precision editing with the Trimmer tool.

Hot Tip

To avoid entering Shuffle mode accidentally, you can engage Shuffle Lock by Command-clicking (Mac) or Control-clicking (PC) its button from any other mode.

SPOT (F3)

Spot mode locks whatever clip you're moving to a fixed, user-defined point in the timeline. Click a clip with the Grabber tool or drag in a clip from the clip view window, and upon release you're presented with a dialogue box asking precisely where you want to put it. This mode is especially useful for adding spot effects when working to picture.

Above: Use Spot mode to add spot effects at precise locations.

GRID (F4)

In conjunction with Slip mode, Grid mode is probably the most commonly used mode for music production, because it locks clip movement and the behaviour of the Selector and Trimmer tools to the current timing grid resolution. This is a way to ensure that your edits are always perfectly in time with the track.

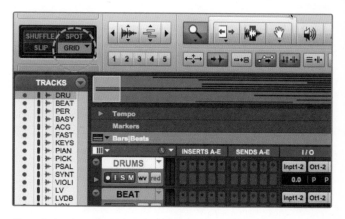

Above: Grid mode excels when arranging your song.

EDITING TOOLS

You'd expect an app with a name like Pro Tools to offer a variety of tools, and it certainly doesn't disappoint. Here's a brief look at them.

Above: The Zoomer tool.

Above: The Trimmer tool.

ZOOMER

Use the Zoomer tool to zoom in to a specific area of a track. Just select it and either click on or draw around the area you want to magnify. Holding down the Alt/Option (Mac) or Alt (PC) key reverses the effect.

TRIMMER

The Trimmer tool is used to trim the length of audio clips or MIDI notes. These are non-permanent edits that can be easily undone by dragging back again in the opposite direction.

SELECTOR

Probably the most frequently used tool, the Selector tool is used to place the edit cursor at specific points in a track, and also to make selection highlights across one or more tracks.

Above: The Selector tool.

GRABBER

The Grabber tool can be used to grab whole clips with a single click and drag them around the screen: either horizontally from left to right, or vertically from track to track.

Above: The Grabber tool.

SMART

The Smart tool is a combination of the Selector, Grabber and Trimmer tools, and gives you instant access to them, depending on the position of the cursor within a clip. With it enabled, position your mouse pointer over the middle of the clip, then move it to the upper half of the clip to bring up the Selector tool, or move it to the lower half of the clip to produce the Grabber tool. Moving the cursor towards the clip's start or end point invokes the Trimmer tool. The Smart tool is enabled by clicking the long button that surrounds the three tools.

Above: The Smart tool.

Above: The Scrubber tool.

Above: The Pencil tool.

SCRUBBER

The Scrubber tool enables you to drag back and forth within an audio clip to find an edit point, emulating scrubbing a reel of tape across a playhead. The slower you drag, the slower the playback. With the Edit Insertion Follows Scrub/Shuttle option enabled n the Operation tab of the Preferences page, the edit cursor automatically snaps to the point where scrubbing stops.

PENCIL

The Pencil tool enables you to draw several types of Pro Tools data, including:

- ◯ **Audio waveforms**
- ◯ **MIDI data**
- ◯ **Tempo changes**
- ◯ **Automation**

Down Tools

If a tool's button contains a small downward-pointing black triangle, holding the button accesses extra versions of that tool with different functions to the standard version.

Hot Tip

Holding down the Control key (Mac) or Start key (PC) temporarily changes the Selector tool to the Scrubber tool.

RULERS AND MARKERS

Crucial for navigating your way around your song, rulers and markers make it easy to keep track of where you are.

RULER VIEW

The rulers span the top of the timeline, providing a reference to the position of events within a song. For most music production projects, at least to begin with, you only really need to view the Markers ruler and the Bars/Beats ruler. You can remove the rest by deselecting them from the Rulers section of the View menu, making more screen room in the process.

MARKERS

You can use markers to quickly navigate to certain points of your song, such as the first chorus or third verse, for example. Markers appear as yellow tabs in the ruler, with thin yellow vertical lines extending downwards across the timeline area. Create a marker by positioning the Selector tool at the required point and clicking the small '+' button in the Markers ruler.

Left: Reclaim space by using the Rulers menu to turn off rulers you don't need.

WORKING WITH CLIPS

Audio and MIDI clips are Pro Tools' building blocks. Here are just a few things you can do with them.

COPY AND PASTE

To copy and paste a clip:

1. Double-click or drag with the Selector tool to highlight the clip you want to copy.

2. Go to Edit, then Copy, or use the shortcut Command + C (Mac) or Control + C (PC).

3. Move the insertion point cursor to where you want to place the copied clip.

4. Go to Edit, then Paste, or use the shortcut Command + V (Mac) or Control + V (PC).

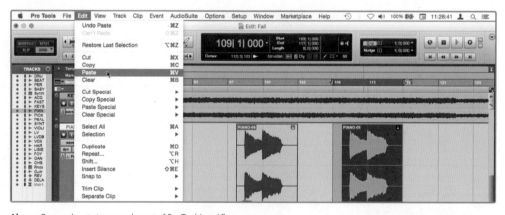

Above: Copy and paste is a core element of Pro Tools' workflow.

NUDGE

Nudging is the technique of moving clips to the left or right along the timeline in precise increments. Use the + and - keys on your numeric keypad for this.

MOVE AND DELETE

To move a clip within a track or anywhere on to a different track, simply click-hold with the Grabber tool and move it to wherever you want. The behaviour of its movement (and where it snaps to when you release it) is determined by which of the four edit modes you're in. Delete any highlighted clips by hitting the Backspace key.

CLIP GAIN

In the lower-left corner of each audio clip is the clip gain adjuster. This allows quick and easy adjustment of each individual clip's volume, useful for making the levels even for clips that have been imported from different sources. To adjust the gain of the clip, just click on the small fader icon and drag it up or down.

Below: Clip gain allows quick adjustments to the level of individual clips in the timeline.

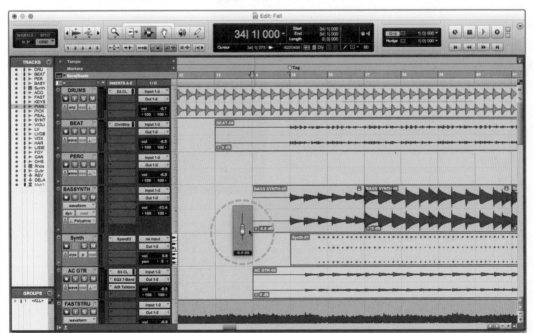

SPLITTING A CLIP

You can split a clip into two in a variety of ways:

1. Use the Separate Clip command. Place the insertion cursor where you want the split to occur and go to Edit, then Separate Clip at Selection, or use the 'B' keyboard shortcut to make the split.

2. Select an area with the Selector tool and, using the Separate command, create a new clip from the selection, separating it from the audio either side of it.

Above: Splitting a clip with the Separate Clip At Selection command from the Edit menu.

3. Clips can also be split by deleting a region within them. Highlight an unwanted area with the Selector tool and hit Backspace. The area will disappear, leaving two remaining new clips on either side.

Hot Tip

To join a split clip back together, drag a selection across the split you want to restore and use Heal Separation from the Edit menu, or Command + H (Mac) or Control + H (PC).

USING PLAYLISTS

In the world of Pro Tools, a playlist is a sequence of clips arranged in a particular order in a track. Each track can have a number of playlists stored within it, but can only play one – the topmost one – at a time. This is great for trying out new arrangement ideas without deleting the old ones.

Above: Creating a duplicate playlist.

Try Out New Arrangement Ideas

To create a new playlist, simply:

1. Click the small triangle button to the right of the track name.

2. Choose New to create a blank playlist or Duplicate to copy the current one.

3. Type a name for the new playlist into the box and click OK.

4. To switch back to the previous playlist, click the button again and pick it from the menu.

DUPLICATING USING THE GRID

Since so much modern music is based on fixed tempos and simple time signatures, Pro Tools' grid makes arranging songs a snap. Literally.

Above: Easily arrange your parts by duplicating in Grid mode.

Copy Sections by Precise Amounts

This arranging technique can really speed up the way you build your songs.

1. Enable Grid mode by clicking its button or using the F4 function key.

2. Make a selection with the Selector tool around the clip(s) you want to duplicate.

3. Make sure the selection is the correct length. For example, to repeat a backing vocal 16 bars further down the song, create a selection range 16 bars long that encompasses the backing vocal clip.

4. Press Command + D (Mac) or Control + D (PC) to repeat the section. The copied clips should be the exact distance of the selection range away from the originals, maintaining their timing relative to the bars/beats grid at that point.

CREATING A BEAT FROM AUDIO CLIPS

Being able to repeat small sections as well as entire chunks of a song can pay dividends when conjuring up beats from single drum hits.

Above: Grid mode makes it a cinch to produce beats from clips of single drum hits.

Program a Drum Track from the Clip List

Use a selection of clips to quickly build a solid groove.

1. Import the individual kick, snare and hi-hat audio files into the clip list.

2. Create three new sample-based stereo audio tracks.

3. Drag and drop the kick drum file into the first track at Bar 1, Beat 1.

4. Change the Grid setting value to quarter notes (*see* page 73).

5. Select Grid mode and make a selection around the clip that lasts for one quarter note on the bar/beat grid.

6. Press Command + D (Mac) or Control + D (PC) to duplicate the kick drum until you have four of them.

7. Repeat for the snare and hi-hat tracks, as shown to the right.

NAVIGATING TIPS

A speedy workflow relies on getting around the interface efficiently. Here are some pointers to help you on your way.

TAB TO TRANSIENTS

Transients are the loudness peaks in an audio waveform that represent the hits in a drum loop or notes in a bassline, for example. They're the transition points from quiet to loud in a recording, and as such are often naturally the points at which you want to make an edit within a clip. Turning on Tab to Transients via its button on the toolbar enables you to navigate to each successive transient in an audio file, by repeatedly hitting the Tab key to move the cursor through the waveform peak by peak.

Left: Tab to Transients helps you locate specific beats more quickly.

Hot Tip

Click the 'a-z' button in the timeline's top-right corner to enable key focus. This means you can use single keys, such as 'R' and 'T' to zoom horizontally.

INSERTION FOLLOWS PLAYBACK

Normally, when you stop Pro Tools and then hit Play again, playback resumes from the same insertion point as before – wherever the edit cursor was when you started playback. In other words, it goes back to where it started. With the Insertion Follows Playback button pressed, playback resumes from where you stopped – in other words, Pro Tools behaves like an analogue tape machine.

Above: The Insertion Follows Playback button.

GRID AND NUDGE SETTINGS

Crucial to navigation, this little box is where you change the resolution of the edit grid. This is the grid that determines where clips snap to when you move them around the timeline in Grid mode. Click on the triangle to adjust it.

Similarly, the Nudge setting determines how far an item moves sideways when you use the Nudge keys.

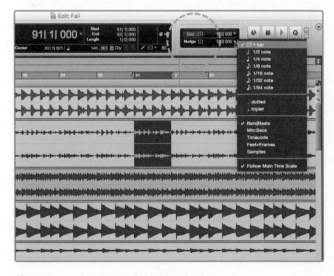

Above: Set your all-important grid and nudge values here.

COMPING

Comping (short for compiling) is the fine art of piecing together the perfect performance from multiple recorded takes.

PREPARING YOUR COMP SITE

When recording a performance that you know will be comped, it's usually best to use loop recording, because this method produces multiple takes of the same part seamlessly, with minimum to-ing and fro-ing. It also enables you to take advantage of Pro Tools' nifty playlist comping feature.

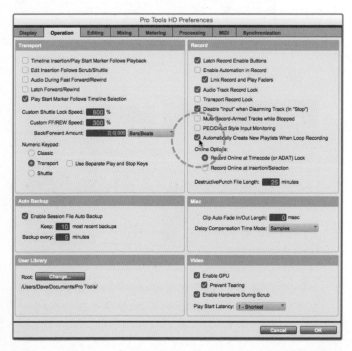

Above: The Automatically Create New Playlists When Loop Recording checkbox.

In order to set this up, take the following steps:

1. Go to the Pro Tools menu > Preferences > Operation, and make sure that the Automatically Create New Playlists When Loop Recording checkbox is ticked in the Record section.

2. Click OK once this is ticked.

3. You can then set about loop recording your parts as described on page 52. Pro Tools creates a stack of playlists, with a different take stored on each.

Putting Together the Perfect Take

So now you have several alternative performances in the can, how do you go about stitching them all together?

1. Once the takes have been recorded, switch the track's display mode into Playlist view. You should see a separate lane for each take, with the most recent on top.

2. Create a new playlist and label it 'Comp' or suchlike. Now the uppermost playlist should be blank.

3. Solo each take with the Solo button in its track header and note any phrases you like the sound of.

4. Draw a selection highlight with the Selector tool around the first phrase you want to use.

5. Click the small upward arrow button that appeared in the take's track header when you made the selection. It should promote that phrase up into the Comp playlist.

6. Continue in the same vein until all the gaps in the Comp playlist are filled.

Above: Playlist view enables you to access the stacked takes.

Above: Promote the best sections by clicking the arrow buttons.

ELASTIC AUDIO

Elastic Audio changes the duration of audio without affecting its pitch. It's enabled by activating one of the types of Elastic Audio plug-in available in each track's header.

ELASTIC AUDIO PLUG-IN TYPES

You can choose from five different Elastic Audio plug-ins, depending on the type of source material you're working on:

- **Polyphonic:** This is best for complex, mixed material.

- **Monophonic:** This works well on single instruments such as vocals, bass or flute.

- **Rhythmic:** This is great for drum loops and other rhythmic material.

- **Varispeed:** This links timing and pitch as a tape machine would – speed up and the pitch increases.

- **X-Form (Rendered Only):** This offers high-quality, general-purpose time stretching, but not in real time.

Left: The Elastic Audio plug-in selector.

Change Song Tempo

To change the tempo of an entire session after it's been recorded:

1. Alt/Option-click (Mac) or Alt-click (PC) a track's timebase selector and select Ticks. This makes all the tracks in the session tick-based, so their timing is linked to the session tempo.

2. Go through the tracks and enable the correct type of Elastic Audio plug-in for each by clicking in the grey space next to the timebase selector in each track's header.

3. Change the session tempo by double-clicking the red diamond in the Tempo ruler and entering a new value. Press Return.

4. All audio tracks should now conform to the new tempo.

Fix Wayward Timing

Elastic Audio can also be used to fix timing problems:

1. Change the problem track's view from Waveform to Warp.

2. With the Grabber tool, Shift-click the vertical grey analysis marker on the beat you want to move.

3. This adds warp markers on to either side of the target beat, so you can drag it earlier or later without affecting the rest of the clip.

Below: Warp factor three – move the central warp marker to adjust a beat's timing.

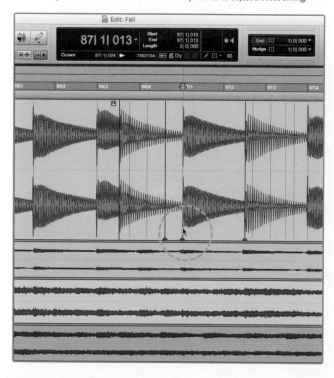

WORKING WITH MIDI

While you can edit MIDI in the Edit window's Notes view, if you need more screen room, Pro Tools also has a dedicated MIDI editor window.

THE MIDI EDITOR

To conjure up the MIDI editor window, just double-click on a MIDI clip in the Edit window.

1. **Solo and Mute buttons**: Isolate or silence the selected MIDI part.

2. **Notation Display button**: Click this to view and edit your MIDI part as music notation.

3. **Editing tools**: Similar to the Edit window tools, but with functions specific to MIDI notes. For example, the Trimmer tool shortens and lengthens notes, while the Selector tool selects them.

4. **Grid mode**: Switch between the four Grid modes, similar in operation to the Edit window modes.

5. **Grid settings**: Changes the resolution of the editing grid.

⑥ **Editing area**: Displays the time position, duration and pitch of each note in the conventional piano-roll style. Notes appear as coloured bars.

⑦ **Bars/Beats ruler**: Marks off the time horizontally in bars and beats.

⑧ **Keyboard display**: Each horizontal row represents a pitch corresponding to a note on the piano keyboard.

⑨ **Velocity lane**: The vertical pegs found here represent note velocity – the taller the peg, the harder that note was played.

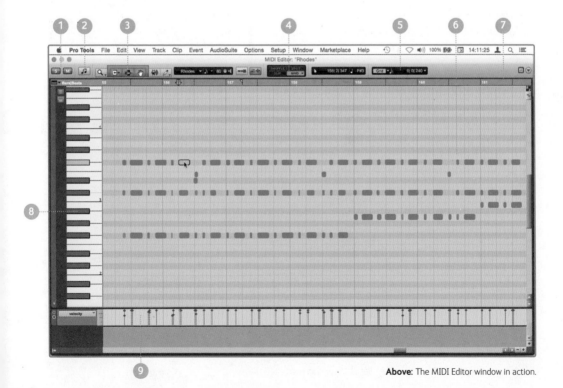

Above: The MIDI Editor window in action.

QUANTIZING

Quantizing is a tool used to fix the timing of MIDI notes to a rigid grid.

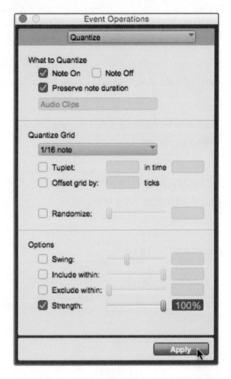

Above: The Quantize window offers a variety of options.

Sorting Out MIDI Timing

To fix the timing of the notes within a MIDI part:

1. Select the target part and go to the Event menu, then Event Operations, followed by Quantize, or hit Alt/Option + 0 (Mac) or Alt + 0 (PC).

2. In the Quantize window's What to Quantize section, click the Note On and Preserve Note Duration checkboxes.

3. Select the appropriate Quantize Grid resolution by choosing a value from the pop-up menu.

4. If required, tick the Strength checkbox and use the slider to select a suitable strength – 100% locks the part rigidly to the grid.

5. Click Apply to apply the quantization to the part.

Hot Tip

Traditionally the practice of locking the timing of MIDI notes to the grid, Pro Tools also enables you to quantize Elastic Audio-enabled audio tracks.

WORKING WITH NOTE VELOCITY

MIDI note velocity is a measure of how hard a note was hit when it was played. Nearly all MIDI keyboards transmit velocity data, and nearly all instruments understand it, translating high-velocity values into louder notes and low values into quieter notes.

Editing Velocity

To edit a note's velocity:

1. Using the Grabber tool, click to select the note you wish to edit in the editing area. It will change colour to indicate it's been selected.

2. The corresponding velocity peg for the selected note turns white. Use the Grabber tool to lift its head up or down.

3. The current velocity value appears in the upper-left corner of the velocity lane as you drag the peg. Release when the desired value is reached.

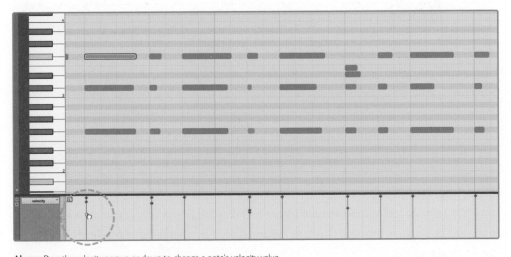

Above: Drag the velocity peg up or down to change a note's velocity value.

FIXING WRONG NOTES

Everyone makes mistakes, but luckily Pro Tools makes it easy to fix a messed-up MIDI performance.

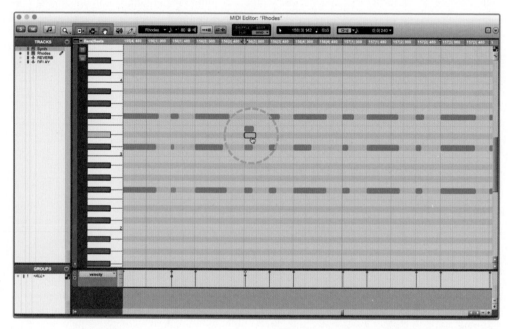

Above: Make wrong notes history with the MIDI Edit window.

Correcting Pitch

Using the Grabber tool, click-hold on the note and drag it up or down to the correct pitch.

Deleting Unwanted Notes

Click on a note with the Grabber tool to select it, then delete it by using the Backspace key.

Changing Duration

Using the Trimmer tool, click-hold on the note and drag either the left or right edge in or out to shorten or lengthen the note. The Edit mode determines whether or not the note length snaps to the grid.

Moving Notes

To move a note, grab it with the Grabber tool and drag it to the desired location. Whether it snaps to the grid or not depends on which of the four editing modes you have selected.

Copy and Paste

Draw a selection rectangle around multiple notes with the Grabber tool to select them. Use the Command + C (Mac) or Control + C (PC) key command to copy the notes to the clipboard.

With the Selector tool, click at the location you want to insert the copied notes and use the Command + V (Mac) or Control + V (PC) key command to paste them in.

Below: Drawing a selection rectangle.

MIXING

MIXING FUNDAMENTALS

Mixing is the process of balancing volume levels, shaping sounds so that they fit together and adding effects to make your track sound finished.

MIXED REACTION

Whenever people see a mixing desk for the first time, their response is often along the lines of, 'What do all those buttons do?' In reality, although it may look daunting, a mixing desk is really just a modest number of controls laid out in a vertical channel, then multiplied to fill the width of the desk. It may be a lot of channels, but they all do pretty much the same thing.

Below: Like any mixer, Pro Tools' Mix window has a vertical channel for each track.

Pro Tools' Mix window is no exception, because it's laid out exactly like an analogue mixing desk, with each vertical channel corresponding to a horizontal track in the Edit window.

ANATOMY OF A MIXER CHANNEL

A basic Pro Tools mixer channel contains these elements:

1 **Insert slots**

2 **Send slots**

3 **I/O (Input and Output) settings**

4 **Automation mode switch**

5 **Group setting**

6 **Pan pots**

7 **Input Monitor/Record Ready buttons**

8 **Solo and Mute buttons**

9 **Channel fader**

10 **Channel Level meter**

11 **Voice allocation**

12 **Channel/Track name**

13 **Delay Compensation settings**

14 **Comments box**

MIXING GLOSSARY

Get to know your inserts from your sends and your buses from your auxes with our whistle-stop guide to mixing terminology.

○ **Automation:** Recording and playing back movement of channel faders and plug-in controls

○ **Aux:** Short for Auxiliary, Aux Input channels in Pro Tools can be used as effect returns.

○ **Bounce:** Export a balance of several tracks to a stereo (or mono) audio file.

○ **Bus:** A path within a mixer down which a signal can be sent to a specified destination.

○ **dBFS:** Short for Decibel Full Scale, the unit in which sound levels are measured on digital systems. Pro Tools' mix channel faders are graduated from minus infinity to +12 dBFS.

○ **Delay compensation:** When you process a sound with a plug-in, the signal

gets delayed slightly. Delay compensation makes sure everything plays back in time.

○ **Fader:** The large vertical slider at the base of each mixer channel that controls the signal's volume.

Above: Insert effects process just the sound within that channel.

○ **Group:** A group of channels linked together so that an operation can be performed on them all at the same time.

Input: The point at which the signal enters the channel.

Insert: An instrument or effect that's been plugged into the channel so that the signal passes through it.

Above: The master channel is the ultimate destination for a signal.

Master: The master channel is a stereo fader that all the other channels in your session are routed to. It routes the audio of your mixed track to your interface's stereo outputs and provides the source when you ultimately export your mix to disk.

Mute: Silence a track.

Output: The point at which the signal leaves the channel.

Plug-in: A software instrument or effect.

Return (or effect return): A channel by which a signal returns to the mixer after being sent to a plug-in (via a send) for processing.

Send: A control that sends a copy of the signal to another destination – usually an effects plug-in.

Slave: A second session at the same tempo as the original session, containing only a stereo audio file of the music, created to increase the number of available audio tracks and ease CPU load when recording multiple vocal, guitar or orchestral parts.

Solo: Silence everything else other than the current track.

Voice: Each Pro Tools session has a finite number of voices. Like tracks on a tape machine, each audio track takes up one voice. Pro Tools allocates voices to tracks as and when they're needed, via a process called dynamic voice allocation.

SIGNAL FLOW

In order to understand the Mix window properly, it's important to grasp the concept of signal flow and the way audio signals move around the mixer.

UNDERSTANDING SIGNAL FLOW

Signal flow is the path an audio signal takes from the input to the output of the mix console. In Pro Tools' case, the input of the mixer might be either the playback from your hard disk (Audio track), audio from a software instrument (Instrument track), or the signal sent from a send via a bus (Aux Input track).

Inserts

Inserts are used to house effects plug-ins that process the audio – for example, a compressor. You can insert up to 10 of these, one after the other, and the signal flows through them in order.

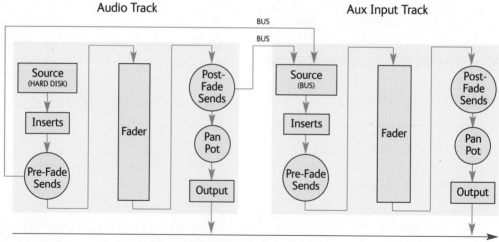

Above: A basic signal flow diagram showing an Audio and an Aux Input track.

Sends

Sends are used to send a copy of a signal to a destination other than the output of the channel. If you imagine that the signal is a flow of water and the mixer is a system of pipes, a send is a bit like a tap. The further you open it, the more signal you let through.

Above: Sends are used to send a signal along a bus to an effect.

Buses

In the same way that a regular bus moves you from one place to another, a bus in the Mix window is a way for signals to travel from a source to a destination. Continuing our water analogy, if a send is a tap, a bus is the pipe the send opens into to send the signal through.

THE MIXING PROCESS – A DUAL APPROACH

When it comes to mixing your song in Pro Tools, there are two different approaches you can take.

TRADITIONAL SEPARATE MIX VS MIX AS YOU GO

This harks back to the days when recording and mixing sessions were completely separate affairs. With all the recording done, all the controls on the desk would be set to zero, and the track would be mixed from scratch, building the mix up a channel at a time.

Because the workflow when producing music in Pro Tools is much more cohesive, the traditional method has largely become overshadowed by the 'mix as you go' method, where the track is mixed as it evolves. This is made easier by Pro Tools' ability to save all levels, effects and automation data along with the session and audio files.

Left: The recording and mixing processes often occur side by side.

LEVELS AND VOLUME

The main idea of mixing is to balance the individual volume level of each track in such a way that everything can be heard in the mix.

Start as You Mean to Go On

Whichever of the two aforementioned approaches you're using, the most logical place to start your mix is with the drums.

1. Create a Master Fader track for the session and either push up the drum channel faders if starting from scratch, or mute everything else if not.

2. Set the master channel fader to unity (0 dB) and balance the drum faders so that the levels on the master channel are reading somewhere between -6 to -9 dB.

3. Next, add in the bass instruments, followed by guitars, keyboards and suchlike, building up your mix one element at a time. Vocals are usually saved for last.

Right: Most mix engineers begin with the drums.

GROUPS AND SUBMIXES

Grouping and submixing are two very useful mixing techniques – but what's the difference?

GROUPS

Groups are collections of channels that can be combined and then edited or affected as one channel. Pro Tools uses two types of groups: Edit groups in the Edit window and Mix groups in the Mix window. They can be turned on or off by clicking on their names in the Groups window in the lower-left corner of both the Edit and Mix windows.

SUBMIXES

A submix is a collection of channels of a similar nature all routed to a stereo Aux Input track. One example would be to put all the drums together into a submix, or maybe all the backing vocals, so that their overall level in the mix could be changed via a single fader without affecting the relative levels between all the channels in the submix.

Left: Solo one track in a group, and the rest follow suit.

THE STEREO IMAGE

From hard left to hard right and everywhere in between, the stereo soundstage sets the aural scene for your track.

PANNING FOR GOLD

When mixing, the placement of each element within the stereo image is arguably as important as its volume level; get the panning wrong and the result can be an uncomfortable listen. The pan pots in the mixer channels give you a wide degree of control, but it's important not to get too carried away with them.

As a general rule, the kick and snare drums, along with the bass, should remain solidly centred, as should the lead vocal and any lead lines. Stereo interest can come from things such as percussion, tracked guitars, stereo keyboard sounds, stereo effects and backing vocal stacks.

Below: Pan pots dictate the position of a sound within the stereo image.

SENDS AND RETURNS

Auxiliary sends and returns form the basic routing structure of any mixer. Here's how to configure them in Pro Tools.

EFFECT SENDS

Effect sends are used to send variable amounts of a signal to an effect somewhere else in the mixer. They're useful when you want to apply the same effect to multiple tracks – for example, putting the same reverb plug-in on more than one vocal track to save processing power.

Setting Up an Auxiliary Effect Send

Each Pro Tools channel can have up to 10 sends enabled. These are labelled in two groups of five, A-E and F-J.

1. Enable the Sends A-E option from either the Edit Window Views menu in the Edit window, or the Mix Window Views menu in the Mix window. This reveals the first five of the 10 send slots available per channel.

2. Click the first empty slot on the channel to which you want to apply the effect. Choose the first available bus from the menu.

Left: Setting up a send in the Mix window.

MANY HAPPY RETURNS

When using a plug-in on an Aux Return, it's common practice to set the wet/dry mix (the balance between the effected and uneffected signal) to 100% wet, because the dry signal still appears at the original channel. The fully wet effect appears at the Aux channel's fader, where it can be blended into the mix alongside the original.

Configuring Aux Inputs as Effect Returns

When you send a signal to a plug-in via a send, it has to return somewhere. This is one of the main uses for Aux Input channels.

1. Create a new stereo Aux Input track.

2. Set the Aux channel's input to be the same bus you selected when setting up the send.

3. Click the Aux channel's first empty insert slot.

4. Select the required plug-in from the menu.

Above: Using a plug-in on an Aux Input channel as an effect return.

5. On the channel you're sending from, turn up the send's fader to send the signal to the plug-in.

6. The effected signal appears as the output of the Aux channel.

APPLYING EFFECTS

Effects bring your mix to life by changing the sound of your audio and instrument tracks. Pro Tools offers a generous selection of effects plug-ins to choose from.

WORKING WITH PLUG-INS

Plug-ins can be thought of as the software equivalent of the racks of outboard gear found in traditional recording studios.

Above: Inserting a plug-in on to an Audio track in the Mix window.

Insert Effects vs Bus Effects

There are two different ways you can use plug-ins: either as insert effects, loaded into a channel's insert slot; or as bus effects, inserted into an Aux Input channel, to which signals can be sent along a bus via sends from various channels. The insert method is best for things such as compressors and noise gates, which need to process single signals, while the bus method works better for ambient effects, such as reverb and delay, which can be applied to multiple channels at once.

Loading Plug-ins as Insert Effects

To load a plug-in directly on to a channel:

1. Tick the Inserts A-E option in the Edit or Mix window's View menu.

2. Click the first empty insert slot in the channel to bring up the plug-in menu.

3. Choose a plug-in from the menu.

Setting Up Plug-ins as Aux Effects
See pages 96-97 for details of how to do this.

USING PLUG-IN WINDOWS
To open a plug-in window and access its controls, just click its button in the insert slot.

Take Control
To use a plug-in's controls, click and drag on the required knob or slider to change its value. Alternatively, for extra precision, you can single-click the value field and type in a new value. As for buttons, just click to enable or disable them.

Loading Presets
No matter what plug-in is loaded, the plug-in window header always features the same controls. Most plug-ins come with some factory presets that can be accessed by clicking the Preset pop-up menu. Just select a preset to load it.

Above: All plug-in windows in Pro Tools have the same header controls.

Target Button
Normally, Pro Tools lets you have only one plug-in window open at a time. Click the target button to be able to open multiple windows simultaneously.

DYNAMICS PROCESSORS

Dynamics processors work on a sound's volume level, and include things like compressors, limiters, noise gates and expanders.

Compressors

Compressors smooth out erratic volume levels, making tracks easier to place in a mix. There's more about how they work on page 102.

Limiters

Limiters are compressors with an extreme ratio setting, so they compress more severely, limiting a signal's dynamic range such that the output level never exceeds a set threshold. Good for preventing clipping.

Noise Gates

Noise gates shut out unwanted noise by muting any audio below a set threshold level. Gates are also great fun to use creatively, because they can be triggered from tracks other than the one on which they're placed to produce rhythmic patterns.

Expanders

Expanders function the opposite way to compressors, widening a signal's dynamic range so that quiet sounds become reduced in level below a certain threshold.

Left: Avid's Channel Strip mimics the company's ultra-high-end System 5 console's EQ, dynamics, filter and gain effects.

SPECIAL EFFECT PROCESSORS

This type of processor modifies the sound in some way, either by adding ambience like reverb and delay, or by completely altering the tone.

Reverb

Probably the most commonly used effect, reverb adds simulated ambience to a sound, making it seem as though it's in a particular space or environment.

Delay

Delay adds a spaced-out feel to a sound by delaying the input signal and reproducing it later, at a time interval set by the user.

> ## Hot Tip
>
> **Don't reserve distortion effects just for guitars – they can work wonders on keyboards, bass and even drums.**

Distortion

Distortion effects aren't just limited to the sort of fuzzy growl you get when you crank up a guitar amp. Much more subtle effects can be had from the distortion stable, such as gentle valve distortion, overdrive and tape saturation.

Modulation Effects

These include things such as chorus, flangers, phasers, tremolo and vibrato effects. Essentially anything that changes the sound with a regular frequency over a period of time.

Right: The AIR Flanger is a type of modulation effect.

COMPRESSION BASICS

Compression can be used either as a tool or as a special effect, but how does a compressor actually work?

A NOTE ABOUT COMPRESSION

A compressor evens out excessive changes in volume level by reducing a signal's dynamic range – the overall difference in level between the loudest and quietest bits. It does this by reducing the volume of everything above a certain threshold by a certain amount (the ratio), then bringing the overall level back up again so the quiet bits can be heard more easily, but the loud bits are as loud as they were before.

Below: Pro Tools' workhorse Dyn3 Compressor/Limiter in action.

The Threshold and Ratio controls are set by the user, as is the amount the volume is raised after compression – the Makeup Gain. You can also control the speed at which the effect kicks in and dies off again with the Attack and Release controls.

EQ BASICS

Short for equalization, EQ is the tool for shaping the tone of your sounds. If you want to cut the bass or boost high frequencies, EQ is what you need.

A NOTE ABOUT EQ

EQ shapes the tone of your sound by cutting and/or boosting selected frequencies within the audio spectrum. For instance, use it to adjust the bass, ramp up the brightness, or remove muddiness from the lower-mid range. You can usually shape the width of frequencies affected by each cut or boost with the Q control – the narrower the Q setting, the smaller the range of frequencies affected.

Pro Tools provides a selection of EQ tools, but the standard issue tool is the excellent EQ3-7band plug-in. This is known as a 7-band parametric EQ, because it offers control over seven separate and variable frequency bands.

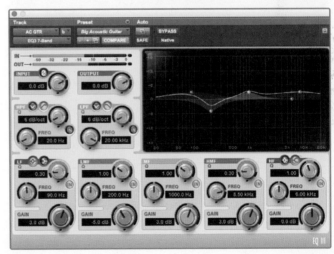

Right: Pro Tools' EQ3-7band parametric EQ throwing some shapes.

REVERB AND DELAY

Somebody call an ambience! Reverb and delay effects are what you turn to when you need a little space.

Above: Pro Tools' Mod Delay III combines a sophisticated stereo delay with modulation effects.

REVERB

Clap your hands in an underground car park and what you hear is reverb – reflections of sound bouncing off the surfaces around you. Reverb plug-ins set out to emulate the sound of these reflections in software, giving you the power to put yourself and your tracks in a multitude of different spaces.

DELAY

Delay differs from reverb in that the effect is made up of individual, delayed repeats of the original sound. Varying the time between the original and delayed signals can have differing effects. Delay times in the order of 10 milliseconds or so have a phasing, chorusing effect, while longer times start to be discernible as actual repeats. These are often synced to the song tempo for ear-catching rhythmical effects.

Hot Tip

Begin your mix session with one global reverb and one global delay, each on its own send and return, so you can send any track to them when needed.

MIXING TIPS AND TRICKS

Mixing can be tricky, but here are one or two pearls of wisdom to help you get the most from your mix session.

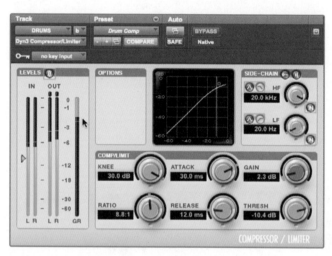

Above: A compressor's gain reduction meters tell you how hard it's working.

COMPRESS TO IMPRESS

When setting your compressor's threshold level, aim so that only the loudest bits are making the gain reduction meters flash, then compensate for the drop in volume by turning up the Makeup Gain by the maximum amount of gain reduction indicated.

A/B YOUR MIX

Compare your mix often to a reference track that you know sounds good. Granted, the song you choose will have been professionally mastered, but it's still a useful guide.

GENTLY DOES IT

Mixing can be a tiring process, so try to take a break every hour or so to let your ears recover. Also, monitoring at a moderate volume level is far less wearing for long periods, and can reveal far more detail than having your speakers cranked up all the time.

AUTOMATION

Bring your tracks to life! Create more dynamic and involving mixes with a touch of automation.

VOLUME AUTOMATION

Automation enables you to add movement to your mix by programming changes – not just in volume but in other controls as well – that occur as the song plays back. As an example of volume automation, here's how to program a simple fade-in on a track:

1. Click the small triangle at the bottom-left edge of a track's header in the Edit window to open an automation lane.

Below: Programming a simple fade-in with an automation curve.

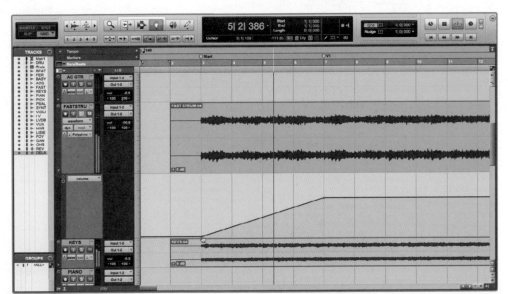

2. Grab the lane's bottom edge and drag it downwards to expand the lane to a decent depth.

3. With the Grabber tool, click on the horizontal black line – the automation curve – to place a node at the point where you want the fade-in to end.

4. Drag the node at the front of the curve down to zero and press Play.

PLUG-IN PARAMETER AUTOMATION

As well as placing nodes on an automation curve, you can record changes to plug-in parameters using the automation mode selector in the mixer channel.

1. To begin, go to Mixing, then Preferences, and select the Plugin Controls Default to Auto-Enabled option. This makes the automation system recognize any plug-in's controls automatically.

2. Insert the required plug-in on the channel and open its control panel.

3. Switch the channel's automation mode selector from Read to Write. All automatable controls should now be lit with small red LEDs.

4. Press Play and move a control as the song plays. All movements are recorded.

5. Press Stop and reset the automation mode switch to Read.

6. Your recorded movements will now be played back.

Above: Recording in automation data from a plug-in control panel.

BOUNCING TO DISK

It's the final bouncedown – but what settings do you use when rendering your finished mix to disk?

Above: Use the Disk option from the File menu's Bounce section to bounce your finished mix.

WHAT IS BOUNCING?

Bouncing is Pro Tools-speak for exporting or rendering your mix to a stereo audio file ready for mastering and/or distribution.

Bounce Away

Once your track is mixed, go to the File menu > Bounce > Disk to bring up the Bounce window. This is where you enter the settings for the bounce.

If you can, always bounce your mix at the same sample rate and bit depth as the session (you can check this in the Session window under Setup). This maintains the fidelity of your audio by not subjecting it to any unnecessary conversion processes at this stage.

By default, the bounce ends at the last audio waveform or MIDI note in the session.

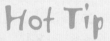

Leave headroom for the mastering process by having your master outputs peak at no more than around -9 to -6 dBFS.

THE BOUNCE WINDOW

This is where you set up everything to do with the type of audio file you're about to create when bouncing your finished mix to disk.

Bounce Source: To bounce a mix, select your system's main stereo output here.

File Type: Choose from WAV, AIFF or MP3.

Add MP3: Bounce an MP3 file at the same time as a WAV or AIFF file.

Format: Choose to export either multiple mono files or a single interleaved stereo file.

Bit Depth and Sample Rate: Choose the same settings as the session if possible.

Import After Bounce: Tick to import the bounced file back into your session.

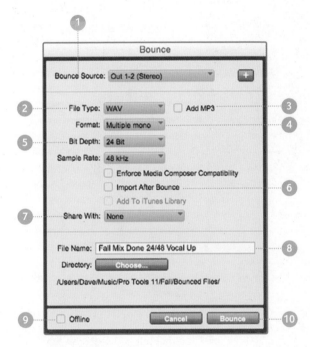

Above: The Bounce window.

Share With: Option to upload interleaved files directly to SoundCloud.

File Name and Directory: Choose where to save your mixed audio file and what to call it.

Offline: Offline bounces are faster than real time, because you don't monitor the audio as the bounce happens.

Bounce: Click this to bounce your mix to disk.

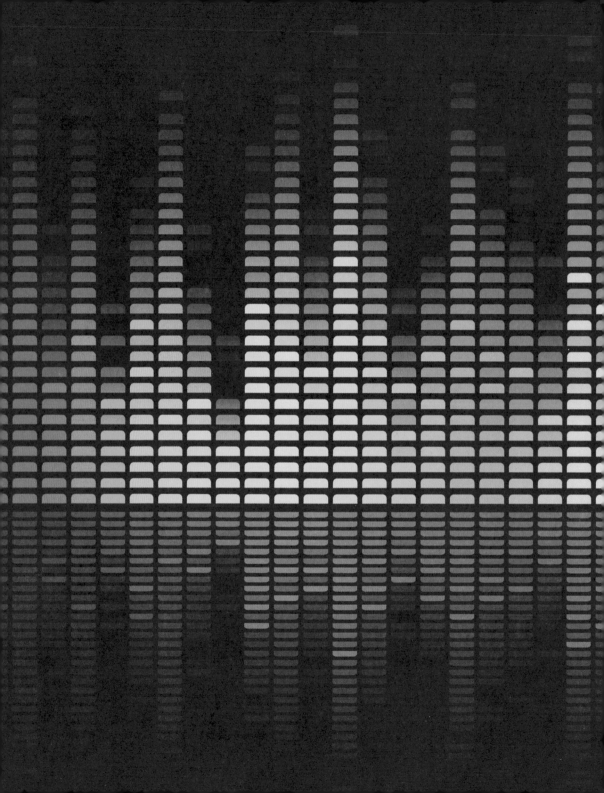

MASTERING

MASTERING BASICS

So now you have a stereo audio file of your mix. What next? Time to delve into the mysterious world of mastering.

WHAT IS MASTERING?

Mastering is the final process that a mixed recording goes through prior to its release. The term was originally derived from the physical process of cutting a master disc from which all copies would later be made for distribution. Nowadays, mastering usually involves taking the finished stereo mix of the song and subjecting it carefully to EQ, dynamics and stereo image processing

Below: Mastering more than one song in the same session ensures a cohesive sound between songs.

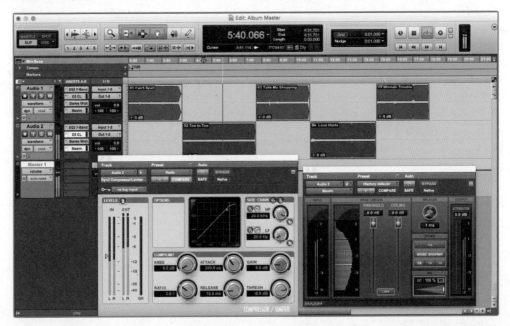

to ensure that it sounds the best it possibly can when played in all environments, from club speakers to the headphones on an MP3 player.

Give It a Go

Although usually the preserve of the professional mastering engineer, the inclusion of all the necessary tools for mastering in Pro Tools' toy cupboard means that there's never been a better opportunity to have a go yourself.

MIXING FOR MASTERING

If you know that you'll be mastering your track in Pro Tools, there are one or two things to bear in mind when preparing to bounce your mix.

1. Remove any master fade-in or -out at the beginning or end of the track, so as to avoid adversely affecting any dynamics processing in the mastering session. The fades can easily be reapplied at the mastering stage.

2. Likewise, remove any EQ or compression across the master channel, because you'll want to reapply these at the mastering stage too.

3. In the Bounce window, choose multiple mono as the format, to avoid having to convert from interleaved when you reimport your audio into the mastering session.

Below: Remove plug-ins from your master channel before exporting your mix to be mastered.

SETTING UP A MASTERING SESSION

Once your track is mixed, close down the mix session and create a new blank session in Pro Tools.

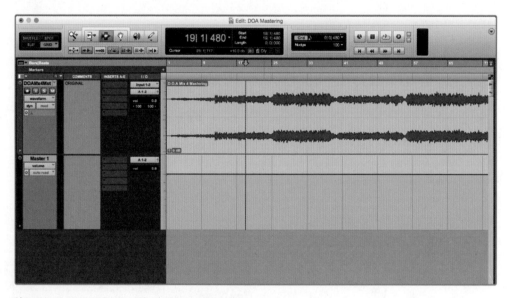

Above: A new mastering session, with a track imported and ready to master.

One thing you need to ask yourself at this point is: how will your music be distributed once it's mastered? For example, CD copy houses require a 44.1 kHz sample rate and a bit depth of 16.

The Right Format?

If you have a particular destination in mind for your mastered piece, it's important to check whether any particular format is required before you create your mastering session. Otherwise, use the same sample rate and bit depth settings as you used in your mix session – 24-bit masters with no mix bus EQ or compression are usually favoured.

Once you've created your session, import your mixed song on to a new stereo audio track, as described on page 56.

REFERENCE AUDIO

To give yourself a target to aim for when mastering, import an audio file of a commercially mastered track that you like the sound of into your session, and run it alongside your mix. Solo them one at a time to compare the sound. This is known as A/B-ing.

Above: Use a commercially mastered track to reference against.

Equal Loudness

The human ear naturally leads us to believe that louder is better when it comes to audio. To avoid being led astray by this phenomenon when A/B-ing, it's important to balance the perceived volume of the reference track against the one you're working on, so that you don't just think it sounds better because it's louder. Do this by reducing the clip gain (*see page 68*) of the reference track until the two sound equally loud. Use the track meters to guide you if needed.

Hot Tip

Duplicate the original mix and run the duplicate alongside the copy you're working on, so you can compare the effect of any processing you've added.

MASTERING EFFECTS

In this section, we focus on how some of Pro Tools' built-in plug-ins can be used in a mastering context.

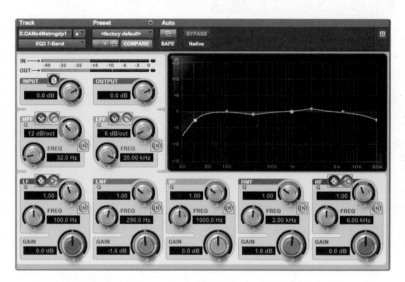

Above: Use a gentle EQ curve to subtly enhance the overall sound of your track.

MASTERING EQ

Mastering is all about trying to improve the overall sound of the mix, rather than the individual elements you focused on during mixing, so it's natural that a decent parametric EQ should be part of the process, and Pro Tools has one in the shape of the EQ3-7band plug-in.

Listen to the overall tone of your mix in comparison with your reference track and, remembering to keep it subtle, use the EQ to round out the bottom end (below 200 Hz), tighten up the mid range (200 Hz to around 4 kHz) or add energy to the highs (5 kHz and above) as required.

Linear Phase EQ

If you can, invest in a decent linear phase EQ, not just for mastering purposes, but for general use. Unlike conventional EQs, these adjust the volume levels of specific frequencies in a signal without affecting the phase of those frequencies.

MASTER BUS COMPRESSION

Some gentle compression, with relatively slow attack and release times to preserve transients and keep a lid on the sustained elements of your mix, is usually all that's necessary when mastering a well-balanced track

Broadband vs Multiband Compression

When mastering a track with a single stereo master bus compressor, this is known as broadband compression. Here, you're looking to see an average gain reduction of only around 1 to 2 dB, so keep the ratio at a gentle setting of around 1.5:1. Makeup Gain should also be around 1 to 2 dB.

To compress a particular frequency range, such as compressing the bass while leaving the high frequencies unaffected, you need a third-party multiband compressor, such as the Waves C6.

Above: The Waves C6 multiband compressor can home in on specific frequencies.

MASTER LIMITING

Once the track has been tonally and dynamically balanced using EQ and compression, limiting should really only be considered as the final stage in the process, just to skim off the peaks and bump up the overall perceived loudness to a commercially competitive level.

Pro Tool-box

Pro Tools offers a choice of tools for this: the standard Dyn3 Compressor/Limiter offers five limiter presets with ratios ranging from 20:1 to 100:1, while the Maxim plug-in also features a peak limiter mated to a dithering and noise-shaping section (see page 123). Maxim's limiter has an unusual automatic Makeup Gain feature linked to the Threshold setting – the lower you set the Threshold, the louder your track gets, so proceed with caution!

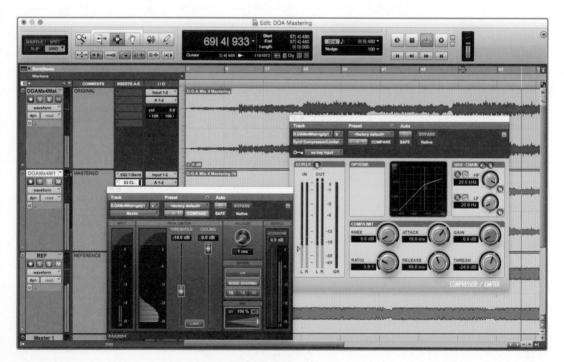

Above: Both the Dyn3 Compressor and Maxim have limiting capabilities.

STEREO PROCESSING

Although decisions on where to place elements within the stereo image should ideally be made during the mixing stage using the pan controls, it is possible to enrich the overall stereo width of a track after it's been mixed.

Wider Still and Wider

Pro Tools' AIR Stereo Width plug-in (found in the Sound Field plug-in menu) uses tiny delays and phase shifting between the left and right channels to create a perceived increase in stereo width.

Mid/Side Processing

This technique enables you to treat the central, mono information in a mix separately from the wider, stereo information at the sides. It's a handy tool for balancing out the stereo image, and the AIR Stereo Width plug-in's Adjust mode uses it to full effect, specifically to adjust the width of an existing stereo signal, such as your mixed track.

Above: The AIR Stereo Width plug-in. It does what it says on the tin.

MASTERING TIPS

Mixing and mastering are two completely different disciplines. Here are a few things to bear in mind when mastering your first project.

○ **Be objective**: Try not to listen to your mix all the way through at the start of the mastering session. If you listen to four minutes of music before you make any changes, you'll have got too used to the way it sounds.

○ **Don't reach for the presets**: If you're lucky enough to own a dedicated suite of mastering tools, such as iZotope's Ozone, don't be swayed by the temptation to just slap on a preset. Even though it might sound great, the presets are only designed to be used as starting points and then adjusted to fit your track.

○ **Save your settings**: Save the plug-in settings you use to master each track as a preset containing the track's name. This can help maintain a cohesive overall sound if you're mastering more than one track at a time.

Hot Tip

In Pro Tools HD, switch from peak to RMS meters. These give an average loudness readout that's more in line with how our ears perceive loudness.

Below: Use the plug-in window header menu to save settings as presets.

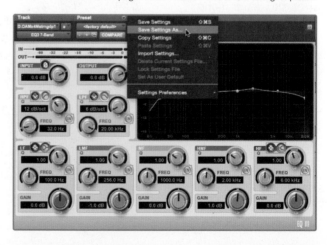

TRIMMING AND FADING

When preparing your mix for mastering, don't be overly concerned if there are portions of dead space or background noise before and after your track. These can often be useful during the mastering process for teaching your track's noise profile to a noise reduction plug-in, such as iZotope's RX4.

Topping and Tailing

If it should happen that your track needs a trim, zoom in close to the point at which the track starts and either use the Trimmer tool in Slip mode to position the left edge of the clip precisely at the required point, or place an insertion cursor with the Selector tool, separate the unwanted region and delete it with the Backspace key.

As for the other end, a good tactic is to program a fade-out on the master channel fader using volume automation (see page 106).

Below: Trimming the start of a stereo audio file.

RENDERING TO DISK

Although similar to the process of rendering a mix file, there are one or two things to remember when exporting your master to disk.

OFFLINE VS REAL TIME

Up until recently, the only option when exporting a mixed or mastered track in Pro Tools was a real-time bounce, in which the song would play back in real time as the audio was being written to disk. While this had the advantage of enabling the engineer to listen out for problems as it progressed, it was also fairly time-consuming and processor-intensive.

Current versions of Pro Tools now offer a swifter option in the form of offline bouncing, in which the computer doesn't bother playing back any audio, and just crunches the numbers required to actually write the data. This makes for a quicker and less strenuous process.

Below: The Bounce window showing settings for mastering to CD.

Bounce
Bounce Source: A 1-2 (Stereo)
File Type: WAV   Add MP3
Format: Interleaved
Bit Depth: 16 Bit
Sample Rate: 44.1 kHz
Enforce Media Composer Compatibility
Import After Bounce
Add To iTunes Library
Share With: None
File Name: DOA CD Master
Directory: Choose...
/Users/Dave/Music/Pro Tools 11/DOA Mastering/Bounced Files/
Offline   Cancel   Bounce

Hot Tip

Try to avoid mastering your own tracks as soon as you've mixed them. Leaving a day or two in between does wonders for your objectivity.

DITHERING

When exporting your master at a lower bit rate than your mix file, you need to add some dither. If the ultimate destination for your track is a CD pressing plant, for instance, you're eventually going to have to downsample (or downsize) your 24-bit master to CD specification – i.e. 16-bit, 44.1 kHz. The process of downsampling to 16-bit from 24-bit invariably introduces some low-level distortion and digital artefacts, so to combat this, a process known as dithering needs to be applied prior to the conversion.

How to Introduce Dither

Dither is simply low-level noise introduced into the audio signal to mask the distortion caused by downsampling. In Pro Tools, you introduce it either by inserting one of the two available dither plug-ins (Dither or POW-r Dither) or the Maxim plug-in into the last insert slot on your master output channel, then specifying the destination bit rate in the plug-in's window before rendering your master.

Above: Avid's Maxim limiter also has a dither function, making it a shoo-in for the last slot in your mastering chain.

SHARING YOUR TRACK

So now you have a finished master sitting on your hard drive, what happens next? There are several options to consider when putting your music out there for public consumption, including:

○ **iTunes**: In the Bounce window, tick the Add to iTunes Library checkbox to add your exported track to your iTunes library. Another option is to upload your master to the iTunes Store (via services such as TuneCore) for people to purchase.

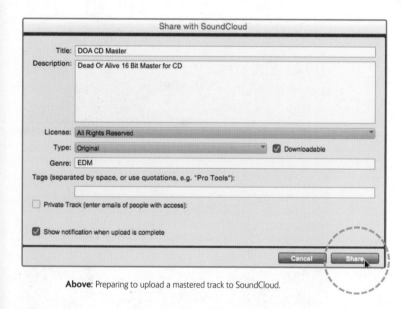

Above: Preparing to upload a mastered track to SoundCloud.

○ **SoundCloud:** As mentioned on page 109, Pro Tools has an option to upload to your SoundCloud account directly from the Bounce window.

○ **MP3:** If you ticked the Add MP3 checkbox, an MP3 version of your track is created alongside your WAV or AIFF version. This can be shared any way you like.

○ **CD:** Although online distribution is becoming the norm, there is still a market for tracks distributed on physical media such as CD.

Hot Tip

When preparing your mix for mastering, remove any fade-out at the beginning or end of the track. These confuse the dynamics processing in the mastering session, and can easily be reapplied at the mastering stage.

AND FINALLY

It's been a long yet hopefully rewarding journey to get to this point.
Now your tracks are finished, why not consider letting an expert pair
of ears subject them to a final tweak?

PROFESSIONAL MASTERING SERVICES

True though it may be that we've spent the last few pages extolling the virtues of self-mastering,
it would be remiss of us not to acknowledge that an experienced, professional mastering
engineer in a purpose-built, acoustically treated room with a load of expensive equipment is
far more likely to achieve a better result.

Be Objective

A good portion of mastering is
objectivity, which may be thin on
the ground if you're attempting
to master a track you've spent
weeks working on in the same
room with the same monitors.

Hire a Pro

If you have the budget to hire a
pro (and there are plenty of
online mastering services
available at reasonable prices),
we highly recommend it. You'll
probably be amazed and
delighted by the result.

Below: Regardless of the high-end, specialized gear, a fresh pair of ears
is the main thing you pay for when mastering your track professionally.

USEFUL WEBSITES AND FURTHER READING

USEFUL WEBSITES

www2.digidesign.com/digizine

Plenty of useful archived hints and tips from past editions of the official online magazine for Pro Tools users, Digizine.

duc.avid.com

The Avid Pro Audio Community is the official forum for Pro Tools users.

www.musicradar.com/computermusic

News and reviews on everything to do with music technology, plus lots of free tutorials.

www.pro-tools-expert.com

A website about Pro Tools run by experts.

www.soundonsound.com/

Head to the online version of this recording tech magazine for advice on all aspects of digital music.

theproaudiofiles.com

A great resource of general tips and tricks from professional audio experts.

FURTHER READING

Huber, D.M., *Modern Recording Techniques*, Focal Press, 2013

Katz, B., *Mastering Audio: The Art & The Science* (3rd Edition), Focal Press, 2014

Macdonald, R., *Everyday Guides Made Easy: Mixing for Computer Musicians*, Flame Tree Publishing Ltd, 2015

Owsinski, B., *The Mixing Engineer's Handbook*, Delmar Cengage Learning, 2013

Senior, M., *Mixing Secrets for the Small Studio*, Focal Press, 2011

White, P., *The Producer's Manual*, Sample Magic, 2011

INDEX